RICHARD HAMMOND's
Caravans

RICHARD HAMMOND's
Caravans

THE ESSENTIAL LOVE 'EM
OR HATE 'EM GUIDE

First published in Great Britain in 2009 as *A Short
History of Caravans in the UK* by Weidenfeld &
Nicolson

This paperback edition published in 2014 by Phoenix,
an imprint of Orion Books Ltd, Orion House,
5 Upper Saint Martin's Lane,
London WC2H 9EA

10 9 8 7 6 5 4 3 2 1

A CIP catalogue record for this book is available from
the British Library.

ISBN: 978-0-7538-2671-3

Design by www.carrdesignstudio.com
Picture research by Brónagh Woods
Edited by Debbie Woska and Jo Murray
Colour reproduction by DL Interactive UK
Printed in China

An Hachette UK Company

The Orion Publishing Group's policy is to use
papers that are natural, renewable and recyclable
products and made from wood grown in sustainable
forests. The logging and manufacturing processes
are expected to conform to the environmental
regulations of the country of origin.

www.orionbooks.co.uk

CONTENTS

Introduction

I love caravanning as much as, if not more than, anyone else. The exact form that caravanning takes for different folk is a debatable thing. I love to blow them up, other people love to go on holiday in them. Live and let live I say. I mean, I happen to love talking to pheasants, other people like to shoot them. It's that kind of difference in approach and attitude that makes this nation great. Besides which, if we don't have future generations of carvanners buying the things new, where will the stocks of old, cheap ones come from for me to blow up? I'd better write a book to encourage them. I'll name it after that one on Ukranian tractors, that did well.

'I love caravanning as much as, if not more than, anyone else.'

It's full of absolutely essential caravanning information, like why it's very difficult to do 150mph with one on the back of your car and why racing them is good fun. There's a bit of history too, just in case you've always wondered who invented the caravan and where the name comes from.

Lots of people hate caravans but it's just ignorance on their part. Yes, they get in the way a bit but they've also played a big part in history and actually stopped a nuclear war from happening. So being stuck behind one on a narrow road is a small price to pay for survival.

There's even a section on cooking in caravans and there's not a swear word in it. I hope you find this book useful. If not you can always use it to start a barbecue.

Caravanning is one of the world's oldest pastimes. Except that in the beginning it was a way of avoiding death, rather than expensive hotel bills in Devon.

OT 7279

1 History

A long time ago, before Boeing invented the 747 Jumbo Jet, goods had to be transported on the ground on the backs of donkeys or, if you were a really successful trader, a horse.

If you were a really unsuccessful trader you had to carry it on your own back. And when you have people moving cargo around you have people called robbers who like pinching stuff. Very annoying when you've walked for several hundred miles across a desert with heavy bags of spices strapped to your donkey and some bloke with a sword and an Errol Flynn moustache nicks it off you. Even more annoying when you spot the same bloke a few weeks later in the market unloading some cheap spices that 'fell off the back of a donkey, guv'.

Hang on, I thought this was a book about caravans? It is, so be patient. Eventually people got fed up with being robbed and some bright merchant came up with the idea that if traders travelled in groups it might put robbers off having a pop at them. Brilliant.

Eddie Stobart, Britain's best-loved haulage contractor, was inspired by this early company's rigorous employee dress code, but specifies a shirt and tie should be worn instead of a pointy hat.

Many of the goods that you see in our shops come from the Far East and it was the same a thousand years ago. Except that instead of flat screen TVs and PlayStation consoles the goods were spices and rare jewels. Much of the trade went through Persia (now Iran) where the name 'Karwan' was given to the groups of travelling traders. And that's where the word 'caravan' comes from.

Pimp my camel
Most camels look the same so it wasn't long before a strong customising scene grew up. Out of shot are purple neon underbelly lights, a flashing hump strobe and bolt-on buttock extensions.

How the West was Won

Bored with the cold winters and rude New York taxi drivers, many early American settlers decided to pack up and move west to California where they would eventually discover the Beach Boys, the Big Mac and Pamela Anderson.

Great riches awaited in the Californian gold fields and Beverly Hills boutiques, but not before the intrepid travellers had fought their way past hordes of angry Native Americans. Picking up a tip from Persian traders, the Easterners travelled in caravans for protection, but because Americans always have to use another name for something they were called wagon trains.

At night the wagons would be parked in a circle for protection. It often didn't work and many awoke to find themselves with short-back-and-side haircuts and a hatchet in their backs.

They do things bigger in the US. Whereas your Persian merchant would be happy with a donkey or two, the flash Yanks in the top picture have teams of four horses. A pity they haven't spent more time constructing their vehicles as those cloth sides won't stop a Native American arrow. And that dust kicked up by his horses will be seen miles away. Chances are he never made it to LA.

Beautiful paintwork on a traditional Romany caravan. Good job it's pretty because if you get stuck behind one of these you'll be staring at it for ages.

In comparison to the vast deserts of Arabia, Europe is quite small so we never got into the big-scale trade caravans.

Besides, in Britain we were living off turnips and wearing animal skins so those goods that were being moved around the place weren't worth pinching anyway.

The first caravans seen in Britain arrived in the 19th century and were lived in by Romany or Gypsy people. Romanies are thought to have come originally from India and spread out around Europe in vast numbers. The Romanies have their own language and traditions, and have suffered from persecution for centuries.

Romanies travelled and lived in brightly coloured caravans pulled by a couple of horses. Today Romanies and gypsies use more modern caravans often towed by Transit vans. The traditional Romany is not to be confused with blokes who 'have a bit of tarmac left over from another job' and offer to resurface your drive for a hundred quid.

If the pace of modern life is too much for you why not hire an authentic Gypsy caravan and a couple of loyal dobbins and have a relaxing holiday on the road? Loads of companies and individuals have lovely Romany caravans to rent.

For more than the price of a beach holiday in Spain you can spend a couple of weeks trying to get a couple of stubborn horses to pull you around Ireland at 3mph.

You'll experience the traditional life of being crammed into a tiny space with no running water and no proper toilet, and be kept awake all night by the sound of rain on the roof and the horses farting.

By day you'll be staring at a horse's backside as motorists furiously honk on their horns until the horse panics and runs amok. A traditional Gypsy holiday: it's the timeshare salesman's dream.

'I used to be a successful racehorse you know. Now I'm stuck with pulling holidaymakers around who don't even know how to drive. Still, it's better than being turned into glue.'

The Wanderer

An old Victorian gent by the name of Dr William Gordon Stables is the most important person in caravanning history because in 1885 he built the first proper caravan. He didn't do it himself because he was a naval surgeon, and while he was probably a dab hand at sawing off legs, was not so good with plywood, so he asked the Bristol Wagon Works to knock him up a horse-drawn caravan to his own exacting specifications.

The doc called the finished vehicle 'The Wanderer' and a very splendid thing it is as you can see, with styling strongly influenced by a Victorian ice-cream parlour.

Inside, The Wanderer had accomodation for the doctor himself, his coachman John,

The Wanderer parked up for tea at a spot chosen by Foley (in tent), whose tricycle is parked dangerously in the road. Hurricane Bob joins in the picnic, but where is the cockatoo? Bob?

You might recognise this imposing gaff Yes, it's Buck House. HRH Prince Phillip has been patron of The Caravan Club since 1952 and on the 100th anniversary of the club The Wanderer was invited to the palace for afternoon tea. Quite how much time Prince Philip spends caravanning is unknown. Since his missus has a good collection of castles to stay in I'd imagine he's an infrequent caravanner. The tiny caravan below was built for Princess Anne. She has since out-grown it and now lives in a massive stately home.

his valet Foley and his dog Hurricane Bob. Oh and a perch for his pet cockatoo. John's job was to look after the horses while Foley was given the task of riding ahead of The Wanderer on a tricycle to make sure the way was clear and also to act as a scout for suitable places to stop. It's not known where the dog's name came from, but hopefully he was named Hurricane for his speed and energy rather than for an ability to generate large gusts of wind. As any caravan veteran knows, flatulence is the enemy of a happy caravan holiday.

Caravans on screen

The caravan has played an important part on the big and small screen ... It's a cheap prop for one thing.

A caravan isn't just a place for actors to have luvvy chats, put on make-up, 'cast' a few starlets on the couch and escape from the paparazzi. Thanks to its chiselled good looks and magnetic personality, the caravan is often the star itself and in a variety of roles. For instance, it's great for adding misery to a plot line. Caravanning is wonderful for a two-week holiday in the sun in the south of France, but if you live in one full-time in a scrapyard in Doncaster it's not quite so romantic.

Second, caravans are extremely easy to blow up (I expect we'll be back on this subject later) and look very dramatic mid-bang. Finally, caravans can play a romantic lead. What conjures up the thrill and passion of young love better than a couple running away to live in a caravan? Even if it is parked in an old gravel pit. Hundreds of Channel 4 dramas have covered the subject.

Thousands of caravans play a starring role in this Alistair MacLean thriller. I can only remember the bit where Charlotte Rampling removes her top. And that was great.

Caravan of love

Or perhaps not. In *Big Brother 8* the producers brought a caravan to the set hoping the residents would use it for secret trysts and hanky panky. Instead, the caravan was used as a handy place to go and bitch about other *Big Brother* residents. Could have been worse. They might have instinctively slipped into a proper caravan holiday and sat around moaning about the rain and arguing about who made the tea.

Coronation Street

The caravan has even made it onto *Coronation Street*. I'm not a Corrie anorak but I can see some elemental caravan errors here.

1. They've forgotten to bring a car.
2. There are too many people to fit into a caravan and . . .
3. I'm worried about the lifebelt on the back. I mean there's pessimism and then there's lunacy. How badly can things go wrong on a caravanning holiday? Worth a thought though: I wonder if they float? One for future investigation.

Mad Max

This is more like it. This Australian Ford Falcon XB V8 has just penetrated a caravan at 90mph and come off best. The car was called Big Boppa and this sequence in the original 1979 *Mad Max* might just be the origin of my love of destroying caravans. What a beautiful sight: even better than Charlotte Rampling topless.

The Spitfire, Hurricane and Lancaster bomber all helped win the war, but the crucial role played by the caravan is often forgotten.

It's about time this shocking lack of recognition is put right and this is the place. In fact, the caravan had made a major contribution even before Adolf needed sorting out. During the First World War members of The Caravan Club, which had been founded in 1907, joined together and in 1916 sent several caravans to the Western Front to be used by the Red Cross. Then, at the end of the war, the club sent fifty caravans over to France for Field Marshal Haig and his staff to use in the mopping up operation after the Germans had surrendered in 1918.

Phyllis was patient with the refugee children, even when they vandalised her caravan with the new paint sets she'd given them for the holidays.

Interestingly, the German surrender was taken in a railway carriage in a forest outside Paris, probably because a caravan was unavailable at the time. When France fell in 1940 Hitler took the surrender in the very same carriage in which Germany had signed the armistice twenty-two years earlier. The carriage survived until the Germans realised that there was a chance that they might have to sign a second armistice in it so they took it to Germany and blew it up with dynamite. I've destroyed many caravans but have never used dynamite. Anyone got a few spare sticks?

But back to caravans. Field Marshal Sir Bernard Montgomery was a brilliant soldier loved by his men. He made the beret and woolly jumper famous well before Samuel L Jackson and Andy Williams adopted them as trademarks. Monty was the victor at the Battle of El Alamein, which won the Allies North Africa. He planned his campaign from his own personal caravan. Amazingly, Winston Churchill even spent a few nights in it before El Alamein. The cigar smoke must have made a right mess of the interior furnishings.

Monty was Allied commander at the invasion of Normandy and of course brought along his caravan from which he directed the fighting and planned strategy.

Next time you're caravanning in France stand to attention and salute the Field Marshal Montgomery. Hero of Alamein, champion of caravanning.

Monty's caravan
No Caravan Club calendar or embroidered wall hangings for Monty. The Field Marshal decorated the inside of his caravan with portraits of his enemies: Rommel, Keitel and other German generals.

Keeping warm is always a problem with caravan life and Monty (below) wisely wore a thick duffle coat.

Preventing WWIII

The next time you're stuck behind a line of caravans on a country lane – and you will be, you just will – before you hit the horn and fill up the swear box, remember this: without the caravan you probably wouldn't be here.

This is not because you were actually conceived on the well-worn tartan cushions of a battered Webley Trumpet – though you may have been and if so, well good for your parents. But whatever the place of your origin, it is, in fact, absolutely true that you owe your very existence to the noble caravan because it prevented World War Three and annihilation of the human race in a nuclear Armageddon.

You think I'm joking? I'm dead serious. In 1981 the United States Air Force had based 96 cruise missiles at the Greenham Common Airbase in Berkshire. That same year a group of women marched from Cardiff to Greenham to debate the wisdom of using nuclear missiles. The station commander refused their request so the women set up a peace camp at the entrance to the base.

The women lived in very basic conditions without electricity or telephones, but they did have the shelter of caravans. By 1992 the missiles had been shipped back to America. The women stayed on in their caravans for seven more years, camping and campaigning against the arms race.

Extraordinary rendition
Where there's a cause there's a caravan. The CIA were caught flying terror suspects around the world so that they could be interrogated in secret locations. These flights occasionally refuelled at Shannon Airport in Ireland. Local anti-war protestors did the obvious and set up a peace camp with a caravan. It is close to becoming an internationally recognised symbol of independence and freedom of speech, as well as bad cooking and chemical toilets.

Old hippies

Many elderly folk take up caravanning to see the country in their retirement. Not these old folks. They're objecting to basing nuclear missiles at Faslane in Scotland and to the war in Iraq. Once again the caravan plays its part in campaigning against the threat of war. You might not agree with the politics but you can't argue with the spirit. Pass the Jimi Hendrix greatest hits, Ethel.

Campaigning

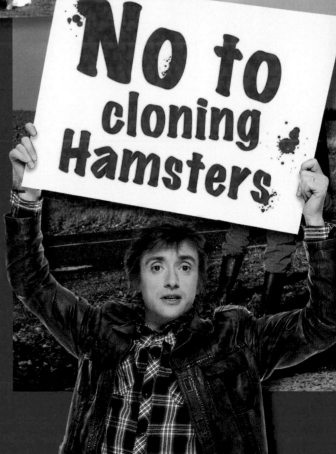

Sisters' sledge
These two members of the Women's Freedom League consider their options after rivals from the 'KWIK League (Keep Women In the Kitchen)' stole their horses. The rotters.

But the women never gave up and eventually they were given the right to vote and the caravan established itself as a weapon of freedom.

It doesn't matter whether you're protesting against building a new airport on your village cricket green or campaigning against the wearing of purple cardigans on Sundays, if you've got a gripe you need a caravan. It's a fact proved by history.

Girls, did you know that it wasn't until 1928 that you got the same voting rights as men? Thank the suffragette movement and the caravan for the change in the law. Campaigners in the early womens' rights movement travelled around the country in a caravan drumming up support for the cause. So missus, when your family expects you to do all the cooking and cleaning up on the family caravan holiday try chaining yourself to the tow hitch in protest. You'll win.

Save our spuds

Genetically Modified Organism. Sorry, but I had to look it up. By fiddling around with DNA and other things with long names and hard to remember acronyms, boffins can make spaghetti grow on trees and all carrots look like rude bits. Actually, I made the last bit up.

Anyway, lots of people considered genetically modified food and animals to be a very bad thing.

So naturally they bought an old caravan that they modified a bit. But not genetically of course.

Caravan racing

No doubt a psychologist will know why it is that man finds racing so fascinating. Racing anything. Chariots, horses, pigeons and even hamsters. God forbid.

But there are few more wonderful sights than a race track full of speeding caravans. I am no professor of physics but even I can see from looking at one that a caravan is not the perfect shape or design for high-speed work. A gentle pootle down to the coast, yes. A brisk sprint across the campsite to get to the best pitch before the Germans, yes. But not hammering into the terrifying Copse Corner at Silverstone flat out.

But physics didn't stop a band of nutters in the mid 1970s from racing caravans at Brands Hatch, Silverstone and several other circuits that could use a ton or two of broken up plywood and kitchen units. Sadly, it never caught on. What a way to liven up a boring Formula One race. If the race became dull the drivers would be waved into the pits and a caravan would be hitched to the back of their cars. 'And it's Hamilton, with the McLaren towing the Dorset Eclipse in the lead as they brake from 185mph.'

The early days
The first caravan races were held under a handicap system. The leading vehicle here is being forced to carry an extra passenger to offset its advantage in having an engine with thirty-five horsepower. The competitor behind has the significant disadvantage of not having an engine at all and only one horsepower.

Oh dear

This well-dressed and keen young driver is clasping his head in panic because he's just spotted his dad sitting in the grandstand. Unfortunately, he'd forgotten to ask permission to borrow the old man's brand new Reliant Scimitar for the weekend. Or the family's equally new touring caravan.

Black-flagged

The race is over for Freddy 'The Hitch' Hitchcock when he's shown the black flag at the end of lap two. Unfortunately, a race official spotted his Great Aunt Ethel waving furiously out of the caravan's rear window. Before you go racing always check the caravan for elderly relatives. An easy mistake.

And they're off

Silverstone has not seen action like it since. Adopt a Murray Walker 1,000 word-per-second delivery and 'they're off. In the lead it's Chris "Camp" Calorgas in the Abbey Strider towed by a 3-litre Reliant Scimitar. My god, he's driving it like he stole it. Then coming up behind is Peter "Pitch" Perfect driving a stunning white Triumph 2-litre towing an ex-Brighton promenade fish and chip caravan. And third pulling up the rear is a blue Vauxhall Cavalier towing a Biffer Springholiday. Oh no it's not, it's a black Hillman Hunter. No it's not, it's a white Ford Capri.' You can feel the excitement. It's high time that the sport of caravan racing was brought back.

Dodgy idea

This shiny red monster is a Dodge Viper. It's got ten cylinders, almost 500bhp and will do over 180mph. Of course, it will easily tow a caravan at a ridiculous speed, or at least fast enough to beat the world caravan towing record of 126.77mph. Easy peasy. Except that there's this thing called drag. Actually, there are two drags. One is dressing up in your mother's clothes and the other is the effect of the air upon a moving object.

More science and the art of going faster

As you speed up the drag slows you down and to go faster you need more power. Despite great bravery, our hero was only able to beat the record by 1.03mph despite having a very sexy car. He beat his fears, but not science. Incidently, towing a caravan at over 120mph is a bit dangerous so don't try it when I'm on the road.

I love science, especially if it's got wheels on it. A Lamborghini Murciélago might have 640bhp but without science it's useless.

A caravan is a rollng science lab and the better you understand physics, the better caravanner you'll be. And safer. If you don't understand forces and gravity then you might stack your six crates of Foster's lager in the rear wardrobe in your caravan and then wonder why the weight came off the back of your car and you crashed in the first corner.

Physics also plays a part in how fast you can go in a caravan. As the brave but foolhardy journalist opposite found out when he set out to break the world caravan towing speed record. Not that I can afford to be too smug about things going pear-shaped at very high speeds. I knew all about the physics when I crashed the jet car. But it still hurt a lot.

It's a drag, but you can't argue with science

Now it's time for a little equation and a bit of maths. Why didn't the sports car tow the caravan any faster? Was the driver wearing too much gold jewellery? No. Unfortunately as you increase speed the power required to go faster is the cube of the speed. So if 10bhp will get you to 50mph in a car, to go 100mph you'll need 80bhp and not 20bhp. Sorry about that, it's science. What our man needed was a 4,000bhp dragster. That'd do the job.

I'm sure that the good Dr William Gordon Stables had lots of lovely holidays in The Wanderer and perhaps even Foley enjoyed the occasions when he was allowed off his tricycle for a pint. But they'd have had even more fun if they'd had a car.

Karl Benz was doing his best. Ironically, while the craftsmen at the Bristol Wagon Works were bashing away on The Wanderer, Benz was putting the first commercially produced car onto the road. Like Romeo and Juliet, Rhett Butler and Scarlett O'Hara, Katie Price and Peter Andre, the caravan and the car were destined to come together in a joyous union. They got hitched in other words.

And as soon as they did people started caravanning. Ships took too long to get anywhere and sometimes hit icebergs, early aeroplanes were dangerous and Center Parcs hadn't been invented so loads of people went holidaying in newfangled caravans. Actually,

Caravan timeline

One horsepower
In the beginning a lot of people had caravans because there was something missing in their lives: a house. Holidays were a bit limited with only a horse.

Petrol replaces oats
Notice how caravanning started getting popular around 1900. Or coincidentally, about the same time as the car was invented. Faster, and no farting.

Spy in the sky
These wealthy caravanners use a spotter aircraft to find suitable pitches that are free from the dreaded working classes. Champagne anyone?

loads of people didn't because you had to be pretty wealthy to own even a car, let alone a caravan. But there were enough people to form a club. Called, would you believe it, The Caravan Club. It's been going since 1907 and in 1908 the club held a rally in a meadow in Surrey. How nice.

The Caravan Club was founded by a bloke called J Harris Stone and to this old fellow caravanners owe an enormous debt. In 1918 they owed him £8 and the club nearly collapsed due to lack of interest. But Stone never gave up and continued running the club through the 1920s and into the thirties. In that decade caravanning really took off with over 100 caravans attending meetings.

The club is still going strong today with thousands of members. They don't blow up caravans or jump cars through burning ones, but then if everyone did there wouldn't be any left for me to explode.

The space age
In the 1950s the world was space crazy. Particularly in America, where everything had to be shiny like a moon rocket. Even caravans. I love this old Airstream van.

Never had it so good
Look at this late 1960s nuclear family straight out of a breakfast cereal ad. Caravans are getting smarter and now even have showers.

Sleek, modern and dull
The modern caravan is designed by a computer and built by a robot. It's efficient, practical and nowhere near as cool to look at as the old 'uns. More chrome please.

From Alberta to Zambia you'll see lumps of plywood being towed along slowly, getting in peoples' way and their drivers sworn at in many tongues.

Next 92 km

2 International

A smallish island with thousands of miles of narrow country lanes and a climate that's as unpredictable as a hormonal teenager, Britain is not the ideal country for caravanning. But we are made of stern stuff and fight our way through rainstorms and temporary roadworks.

We do so because as a nation we love caravanning. In fact, the only Europeans who do more camping than us are the French. Even the Germans, who have an enormous caravan-building industry, aren't as camp happy as we Brits.

But we're not the only ones because everywhere you go in the world sooner or later you'll get stuck behind a caravan. In America it'll probably be about the size of your house back home and more than likely it'll be towed by a pick-up truck driven by a bearded man with a check shirt who is not a member of Weight Watchers but is a lifetime member of the National Rifle Association. Yes, you'll meet many odd folk on the road but they all love caravan life.

The USA

Many people, and Europeans in particular, are very snooty about the fact that only a small percentage of Americans hold a passport and ever go abroad.

Well of course they don't. Why bother having a small but very embarrassing photograph taken when you've got everything worth seeing in your own country? America has got everything from mountains to empty plains, great forests to dirty great holes in the ground, from cattle country to teenage girls on rollerskates on Californian beaches. And, of course, they've got Disneyland.

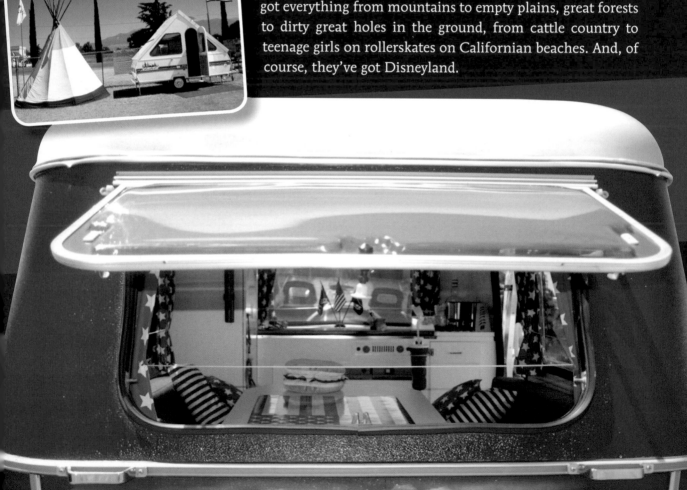

Because Americans speak a foreign language that only vaguely resembles English, they don't call caravans caravans. They call them travel trailers. They do, however, make the world's sexiest travel trailers. Above you can see an Airstream model in all its shiny aluminium glory. Even arty people in Chelsea who wear brightly coloured ties like Airstream caravans.

Some Americans live permanently in caravans and are called 'Trailer Trash', which is also a term of abuse.

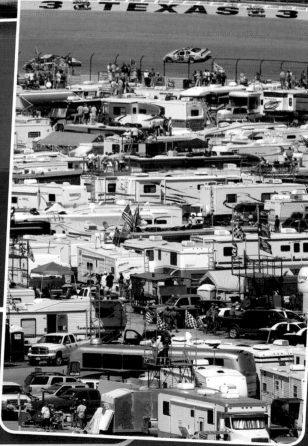

Born to caravan
Many Native Americans prefer to transfer the tradtional shape of the tepee to their caravans (opposite top). Trailer Trash in Texas (right). A classic Airstream in all its shiny aluminium glory (top). So sexy that even I wouldn't want to blow one up. Well, probably not.

Australia

People who live in Texas always bang on about how Europe could be fitted into their neighbour's front garden, but Texas has got nothing on Australia. The country is massive and what's more there's nothing in it.

Paul Hogan, Shane Warne and the cast of *Neighbours* live there but that's about it. The rest are working in pubs in West London and Sussex. Once you leave the east coast and the cities of Sydney and

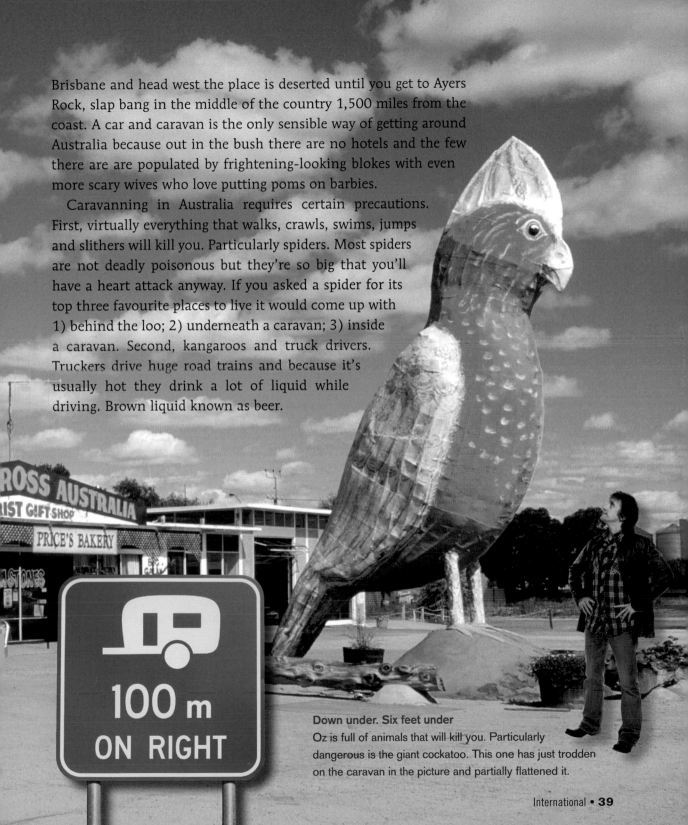

Brisbane and head west the place is deserted until you get to Ayers Rock, slap bang in the middle of the country 1,500 miles from the coast. A car and caravan is the only sensible way of getting around Australia because out in the bush there are no hotels and the few there are are populated by frightening-looking blokes with even more scary wives who love putting poms on barbies.

Caravanning in Australia requires certain precautions. First, virtually everything that walks, crawls, swims, jumps and slithers will kill you. Particularly spiders. Most spiders are not deadly poisonous but they're so big that you'll have a heart attack anyway. If you asked a spider for its top three favourite places to live it would come up with 1) behind the loo; 2) underneath a caravan; 3) inside a caravan. Second, kangaroos and truck drivers. Truckers drive huge road trains and because it's usually hot they drink a lot of liquid while driving. Brown liquid known as beer.

Down under. Six feet under
Oz is full of animals that will kill you. Particularly dangerous is the giant cockatoo. This one has just trodden on the caravan in the picture and partially flattened it.

100 m ON RIGHT

I'll tow if I want to

Towing. This is where the wheels can come off the wagon. Often quite literally. This is a subject we'll be coming to later on in our how-to-do-it section. Just in case you were wondering whether I'd actually get around to offering some useful advice.

Many people are completely put off caravanning by the thought of careering down the motorway with a house attached to the back of the family car by a small piece of metal the size of a pool ball. Towing is actually one of my favourite bits of caravanning, or the bit I like most that doesn't involve a gallon of unleaded and a box of matches. I've driven a Formula One car and that's easy peasy compared to reversing a large caravan up a Somerset lane with two children screaming in the back and all the crowd from the Glastonbury music festival in front of you honking horns.

Mr Davis wonders how to tell his wife that he forgot to have the Land Rover Freelander serviced before the family holiday in Bulgaria. Try going for a run with a wood-burning stove on your back and you'll know what it feels like to be a car engine towing a caravan.

Stationary caravans

This is called a traffic jam and if you practise caravanning in the UK you will spend most of your holiday in one. Now, this looks like a good opportunity to get someone else to drive the car for a bit while you go to the caravan for a kip or perhaps to practise your dart throwing (good for relieving stress).

Two problems here. Firstly, if the traffic moves off suddenly your aim will be upset and you might hit the telly. Second, it's illegal for passengers to travel in a caravan while it's moving. This doesn't apply to animals, but you don't want your labrador playing darts because his paws will damage the darts' delicate flights.

Tow in the water

Easily done. In the panic of packing for the caravanning holiday to land-locked Luxembourg this family has accidentally attached the wrong trailer to the family car. Always compile a check list and tick off each item. Ski boat should not appear on the list. It's also a good lesson in the importance of using your rearview mirror.

Europe

Europe is caravan heaven. Our European cousins are very caravan friendly so there'll always be a warm welcome for you when you arrive at a campsite. You just might struggle to understand the language.

It's the diversity of cultures that make caravanning in Europe so much fun. In only a day's drive you can have arguments with four different nationalities of policeman. There's also a massive variety of different landscapes to enjoy. You can take in the natural beauty of the Alps as you wait for the smoke to clear from your burnt clutch, and enjoy the Italian Amalfi coast in the summer sun as you wait for a local garage to fix the car's burst radiator.

Dutch caravan

The Dutch are enormous fans of the caravan. There are several reasons for this. In the early days of motoring cars had great difficulty in negotiating steep hills and had no chance with extra weight on the back. There are no hills in Holland so that's easy. Also the Dutch have a very relaxed attitude to sex, to which a caravan is a perfect accompaniment as any teenager will tell you. Or adult.

The *Great* Ralph Lee

Who is Ralph Lee? Only the world's greatest caravanner and the only person to be decorated by the Queen for services to caravanning.

Lee built his first caravan in the early 1930s after a very wet honeymoon under canvas with his wife Muriel. He called his home-made caravan 'Who Cares?' and followed it with another ten caravans all bearing the same name. The Lees covered over half a million miles with their caravans and were the first ever allowed into the Soviet Union with a caravan. Although he was a dentist, Ralph designed many caravans and was vice-president of the Camping and Caravan Club. In 1999 Lee was awarded the MBE for his dedication to caravanning and for his contribution.

Ralph was still caravanning aged 96, three years before his death in 2002.

The travelling dentist
Although he pulled teeth for a living, Ralph Lee much preferred pulling caravans around Europe and beyond. Here he is next to a partly constructed hotel in Greece and outside his own home with one of his Who Cares? caravans. Ralph Lee: caravan god.

Festivals

There's a big problem with hotels. Several in fact. They're expensive, often full of boring business people attending a photocopier conference, they're usually nowhere near where you actually want to be and finally, there's the worry of how recently they washed the sheets.

It is far more sensible to take your accommodation with you. Take music festivals, although I'd rather not, to be honest. The great music and scantily clad hippy girls are great, but it's the Western Front at Passchendaele mud that puts me off, especially if you have pitched a tent on it. Much more sensible to bring along a caravan. You'll be dry, warm and you have somewhere to take any new friends you might make at the festival. And it's not just music events where the caravan is king. Whatever your hobby, from sheepdog trials, shows for pre-Second World War static single-cylinder diesel-engined water pumps or naturist gatherings, a caravan will make the event ten times more interesting.

Caravans are owned by people who go out and do things. That caravan you're stuck behind on the M1 could be driven by a bloke who's a world motocross rider or is the top breeder of Weimaraner puppies.

And if you are into heavy rock music, you can throw a TV out of the window just like you would in a hotel bedroom.

Like, totally cool
According to Volkswagen archivist Professor Hendrik von Metallica more babies were conceived in the company's iconic Type 2 van than in any other 1960s vehicle, although Ford is said to be challenging the claim with its MK1 Cortina.

3 Lifestyle

Most of the caravans that I've blown up, set fire to or driven through have not been mine. Actually, none of them have been mine. Obviously.

If I did own a caravan, then thanks to the rather unusual and specific nature of my enthusiasm for them, I probably would blow it up. But plenty of people, having spent quite a bit of money on their caravan choose, for whatever reason, to go on holiday with their family in it.

Which, in fact, can be almost as dangerous because there are dozens of traps to fall into in the world of caravanning. Like arriving at a campsite and choosing a pitch next to a caravan containing an amateur folk singer who plays the mouth organ.

This chapter contains some very useful practical advice such as the trick of finding a decent place to stop for the night (which is called a pitch); what accessories to buy for your caravan to make you love it even more – apart from a rocket-propelled grenade; things to do when it's raining; and the pleasures of celebrating Christmas in your caravan. There's even a section on cooking and how to avoid setting fire to your caravan in the process. Unless, of course, that is your aim. In which case, carry on. And send me a photo.

Buying

Being in the caravan destruction business I have obviously never bought a brand new caravan. I am childish but not stupid. Turning many-thousands-of-pounds-worth of spanking touring caravan into matchwood would be crazy and immoral. Though wonderful to watch.

I can't sleep for excitement when I'm buying a new motorbike so buying something that you can live in and travel the world with must be incredible. Like buying a new house without having to deal with estate agents or solicitors. Of course, you can always buy secondhand and ignore unsightly stains left by previous owners. If you do, then never, ever think about what those stains may be or how they might have got on the sofa.

Old caravans are often very cheap and can be a real bargain. But I'll have probably bought the real giveaways. And burnt them.

Caravan bazaar
No, it's not an over-full caravan park, it's the Caravan Show. The perfect place to find your new caravan. You won't be allowed to stay overnight in one or test the loo but you can see if your kids can destroy it and its fittings. Mine managed it in seconds, the little cherubs.

Top tips for buying used

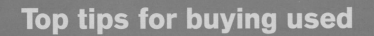

Interior space:
Will your family fit in it? Especially important for Catholic families.

Condition:
Caravans are not particularly tough, which is why it's easy to drive a car through them. Check it's not falling to bits. And that I haven't driven a car through it.

Wheels:
It should have at least two. And an equal number on both sides.

Toilet:
Check it's not blocked and is working. And then never, ever, ever go in there again. Ever.

Here's one I made

STAR BUY!

It can't be very difficult to make a caravan. There's not much to them: just a stack of plywood, a bottle of glue and a bag of nails. Plus a few bits and pieces like wheels, tyres and of course a roll or two of linoleum in gaudy colours that won't show up spilt baked beans and egg yoke. In fact it's so straightforward that I've set up my own caravan factory at the end of my garden. Our first design, the fantastic £250,000 Hammond 2000 is shown opposite in this advertisement currently appearing in Guns and Ammo magazine.

Computer Equipment

THE HAMMOND 2000

It's time that the caravan moved on from being simply a square box with a couple of wheels on it. That's why the technical wizzards at the Hammond Caravan Co's research and development centre (my garden shed) have come up with a caravan for the 22nd century. It's the new Hammond 2000.

Twin rockets
Essential multi-use weaponry for clearing traffic jams, removing caravans from the best pitch and dispersing rain clouds.

Roof llamas
Filling this purpose-built roof rack with livestock provides self-sufficient living and transport to the pub if you can't be bothered to unhitch the car.

Incoming!
Looks like a TV dish but it's actually the Hammond Early Warning Radar System. Predicts weather, missile attacks and whether the M6 is at a standstill near Manchester.

Feel the force
It's important to have weight over the tow hitch. This F1-style wing produces 1 tonne of downforce at 150mph. You can't go that fast of course but at least it looks cool.

Women and children first
The patent caravan escape system not only provides a safe exit from a caravan that has crashed into the sea, but can also be used for recreation and extra bedding.

What's it called?

Thinking up names for things is really difficult. Even babies. You can buy books full of baby names but still Sir Bob Geldof came up with Fifi Trixibelle for one of his daughters.

Caravan manufacturers are the real masters of monikers. The ones they bestow on their creations achieve levels of romance, freedom and optimism not seen since the Lakeland poets were penning their stuff.

One of my favourite motorway games is thinking up new names for caravans. Try it, it's great fun. The following though are real examples of caravan names chosen to capture the excitement and visceral thrill of a touring caravan. The name of the caravan is, after all, going to be written across the back of it and will therefore be stared at by a great many happy drivers following it for a great many hours. So those names are excellent advertisements for the pastime to a captive and doubtless grateful audience.

Animals are a good source of names. How about The Terrier? Rover is an obvious choice but a now dead car company got there first. The Whippet is one of my favourites.

The Hurricane

A worst nightmare is to be caught in a hurricane in a caravan. If houses are blown away your collection of plywood doesn't have a chance. But that doesn't matter in the optimistic world of caravan names.

The Sprite

A sprite is an elf or a fairy. Or, interestingly, a red-coloured flash that occurs in the upper atmosphere during a thunderstorm when high energy electrons hit air molecules. Or when the chip pan catches fire on the hotplate.

The Typhoon

Another windy name. Since typhoons usually occur in the Pacific or Asia you're quite safe in Bognor. Perhaps a shortening of the name to Typhoo would be more suitable for the UK where storms in teacups are more common.

Elddis Firestorm. Are they mad? This is a real name from a real company. You'd think this was tempting fate somewhat.

It's like a boat company calling its new craft the Rickety Capsize or an aircraft manufacturer naming its new airliner the Structural Failure. Another company produces a Meteorite but you're unlikely to be hit by one so that's not so bad.

The weather and the elements do seem to feature strongly in the lexicon of caravan names. Hardly surprising as one of the joys of caravanning must be getting closer to the weather; waking to the rush of raindrops hammering onto the fibreglass roof and then later, drifting off to sleep to the gentle slop of the chemical toilet sloshing as the caravan is rocked on its wheels by the wind off the sea. Romantic and powerful stuff.

But as you'll have seen on the previous page, the names chosen are even more dramatic than our climate. Hurricanes are rare and so are typhoons. As we have established that the caravan's name is a very effective form of advertising, plastered as it is over a very slow-moving billboard resting only inches from the bored faces of thousands of following motorists every year, it's important that the oportunity is taken to convey something of the reality involved in the pastime. And also, a little more honesty would give foreign caravan enthusiasts an idea of what they're in for on a visit to the UK by reading the backs of our caravans as they slump off the ferry in Calais and head for the out-of-town, cheap booze shops.

So I've put my thinking cap on and come up with far more descriptive caravan names that do the job a little better and turn the touring caravan into the British Ambassador it really should be. The possibilities are endless.

The **Windswept Vista** beautifully describes the North Yorkshire Moors or Scottish Highlands with an honesty that takes nothing away from their beauty or appeal as a holiday destination.

How about the **Crashing Wave** for Cornish campers? Second thoughts, you don't want the word 'crashing' in the name.

The **Rain-Streaked Window** will resonate with the thousands who have spent many happy, happy hours staring through one at the couple in the van next door trying, and failing, to light a barbecue. And why stick to the weather? Manufacturers should be braver and let their creative juices flow into other aspects of caravanning and caravans in the UK.

The **Wayward Wanderer** suggests romance and a brave desire to move on, to never let the grass grow under your poorly braked wheels. It also says something about the way it handles on the road.

The **Thrifty Thrombosis**; this tells you that it's usefully priced and reminds you that sitting for hours and hours on a tartan-patterned, Dralon cushion from which you can reach the kettle, the pie-warmer, the door and the lavatory without getting up will, eventually, catch up with your arteries. It's not just a name, it's a useful service to the health industry. Continuing in the same vein, as it were, the **Damp Lung**, the **Trench Foot** and the **Hardly Hygienic** all spring to mind.

What's the hitch?

Unless you're happy to spend a two-week holiday on your front drive you're going to have to tow your caravan behind a vehicle.

And unfortunately this is often where the trouble starts. Matching the right vehicle to the right caravan is very important. Making sure they're securely attached to each other is even more so. A surprising number of people ignore this sound advice.

Size matters

If you car can't tow a caravan bigger than this Portaloo on wheels then it's time to buy a bigger car. But they are out there, the microvans. The smallest ever made was . . .

Well hitched

There's no faulting this gentleman's hitching skills. Note how the car and caravan are still joined together despite the latter being reversed into a Second World War bomb crater.

Poor man's hobby

Caravanning suits all pockets. This old biffer can't afford a car so he's using his bicycle instead. Unfortunately this limits the size of caravan that can be pulled. Still, the terrier can enjoy a nice holiday while his master pedals along.

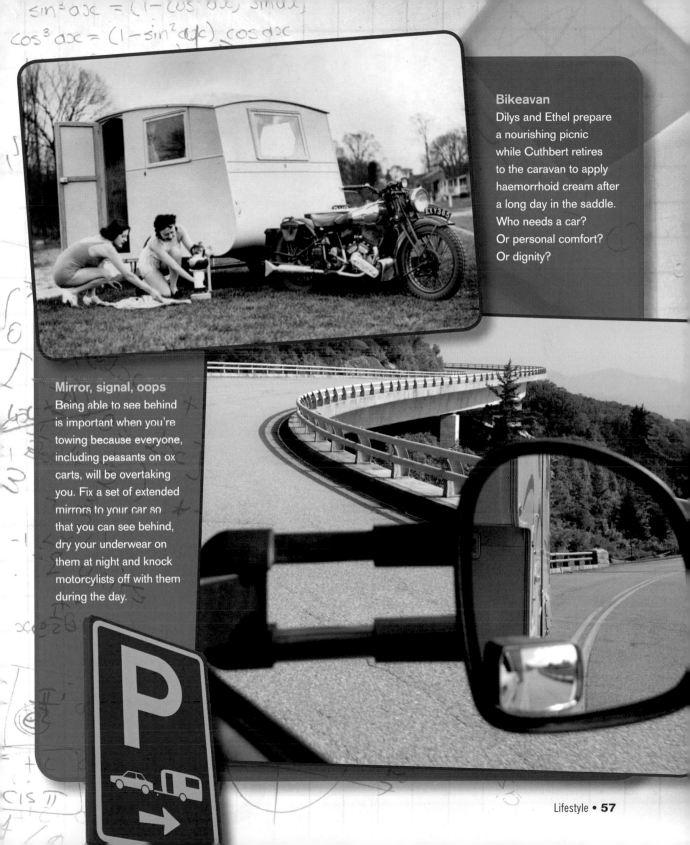

Bikeavan
Dilys and Ethel prepare a nourishing picnic while Cuthbert retires to the caravan to apply haemorrhoid cream after a long day in the saddle. Who needs a car? Or personal comfort? Or dignity?

Mirror, signal, oops
Being able to see behind is important when you're towing because everyone, including peasants on ox carts, will be overtaking you. Fix a set of extended mirrors to your car so that you can see behind, dry your underwear on them at night and knock motorcylists off with them during the day.

What's the hitch?

Towing a caravan need not be a hair-raising experience. It's just a matter of science. Make sure to have plenty of weight on the tow hitch.

Carrying 400 cans of baked beans in the back of the caravan will make the rear of the tow car go light and you might have a dreaded speed wobble. Even if you don't, eating baked beans in a caravan is risky due to the potential gas issues.

Weight balance
Make sure your vehicle is sturdy and strong enough to tow with. There's no danger of this trailer flipping its tow vehicle into a speed wobble. There's no danger of there being any speed.

Wrong again

Remember the family a few pages back that hooked up the wrong trailer and took their boat camping? Here they've done it again and gone waterskiing with their caravan. It was never going to work and I recommend not even trying it.

Double trouble

If you have a big family don't try towing two caravans or this will happen. Buy one big one instead as it's much safer. And reversing will be easier. Only marginally, but easier all the same.

Caravanners the world over spend their lives looking for the perfect pitch. Below is Monument Valley in Arizona. Not far off perfect I'd say.

The perfect pitch

The perfect pitch is the holy grail of caravanning. Some people spend their whole lives trying to find it but never succeed. For many the pleasure is the search, like a Buddhist on his or her path to true enlightenment. Sorry, I'm getting a bit carried away.

But what is the perfect pitch? Good question. My Uncle Cedric was allergic to salt water and sand so a pitch with a beautiful view of the golden sands of the French Riviera would have made him very grumpy (unless it was a nudist beach). If you're into surfing, then Uncle Cedric's favourite caravan park just outside Wolverhampton would be a living hell. You'll be better off on the north coast of Cornwall.Like aeroplanes? Then find a pitch on the landing approach to Gatwick Airport.

Everyone's got their own idea of caravan heaven, which is why over the next few pages we'll be covering every aspect of pitching camp. And that includes many of the possible pitfalls. There are tips on avoiding a bad experience that could wreck a holiday. For example, if you pitch on the bank of a lake and a purple fish rides past on a bicycle, immediately hitch up to the car and get away quick because you've accidentally pitched beside a nuclear power station's waste dump.

Learn to judge your fellow campers from several hundred yards. A morris-dancing costume hanging on a washing line is a clear warning to pitch elsewhere. Nothing wrong with folk dancing, it's the farts from the real ale that are the worry.

Always check on the facilities available on site before you arrive. This is a tip passed down from the great Dr William Gordon Stables, but today you don't need a valet on a trike because we have mobile telephones.

The elderly couple above once made the mistake of not calling ahead to check if power hook-ups were available. Now they always make sure they're within a kettle cord's length of the National Grid. Always learn from your mistakes.

A copy of *The Good Pub Guide* is as essential to a successful caravanning holiday as is bringing a DVD player for the kids. Never pitch more than a short stumble from a good boozer because, apart from drinking a lot of their beer, you'll be wanting to nick their loo paper, too.

You can't beat a good mountain view, but whatever you do make sure the gas bottle is full before you go or you'll be found next season frozen rigid upright in the shower.

You can't beat the peace and tranquillity of pitching beside a lake. I said beside a lake, not in it you fool. Plywood doesn't like the damp so this caravan is now scrap. I can't even blow it up. Second thoughts, where can one buy a torpedo?

This is what I meant. The soft lapping of the water on the shoreline, the sizzling of a freshly caught trout baking in the oven. The caravan lights playing on the ripples across the water and the gentle shrill of birds in the trees.

And all night you'll be scratching mosquito bites.

Now this looks like a pretty good pitch. It's not Clacton-on-Sea. Why? Because you don't get palm trees in Clacton and there's no need for a canopy to create shade because there isn't any sun there either.

OK, so you've found the perfect place to spend a couple of nights with your loved ones, sitting outside in the evening light with a nice bottle of Chablis and some locally sourced food.

Not so fast. You might have a beautiful view of rolling hills and snowcapped mountains in the distance, but what is the actual pitch like? And even more importantly, the neighbours? Pitching camp is an art in itself. For example, judging how far you pitch from the toilet block. We'll be coming to the unsanitary subject of the caravan 'throne' a bit later (I bet you can't wait), suffice to say here that the best option for when nature calls is to use the site's facilities.

Pitch too close to the loo block and, while you'll quickly get to meet all your fellow campers, they will be passing your door with loo rolls under their arms and will probably not be in the mood to stop and chat. Plus you may find that the convenience of the convenience is rather questionable the morning after the campsite's real ale drinking competition.

Too far away is not good either because you might need to find the place in the dark. Having had a four bottles of plonk and a hot boil-in-the-bag vindaloo. Around 100-150 metres is about right.

HILL

Eden Vale

'The peaceful caravan site'

Welcome to *Eden Vale*, a little haven on earth and the perfect place to get away from it all. We guarantee **no crowding, no noisy children** and perfect weather with **no rain** (please see small print and legal disclaimer) and temperatures in the 20s all year round*.

We have a wide range of facilities to make your stay like a home-from-home. There's an entertainment block with a bar so that late at night you'll witness the heartwarming sight of teenagers enjoying themselves.

Please note, Eden Vale has a no-refund policy. Once you've paid for your stay any problems are yours. Don't come complaining to us if your neighbour is playing Motorhead at 120 decibles at three in the morning.

* In our office.

Some people really like to get away from it all. There's not a soul in sight on this moorland pitch.

And for good reason. There will probably be panthers living on it, having been released from a nearby scrapyard in the 1970s. They have since bred successfully and thrived by learning to peel open the flimsy walls of caravans and pluck the slumbering occupants from their winceyette sleeping bags like diners shelling prawns.

And there are further problems to consider if you go for the Ray Mears pitch. For example, how will you describe your location to the pizza delivery boy? 'We're at map reference 052N089W' will be lost on the youth of today.

Lovely pitch. Marvellous view out to sea and only a couple of other campers to disturb this picturesque scene.

Trouble is there's a storm coming and within a few hours the people in that tent will be banging on your door seeking refuge. Send them to the hippies in the van. Always check the weather forecast before pitching.

Ah, wonderful, after a day's drive you've finally arrived at the site that's got the fantastic mountains views.

And so has everyone else. This will happen. Some people claim to enjoy the business of setting up a sort of tenement-slum arrangement of close-parked caravans nestling in one another's shadows, sharing space and bodily smells. I, for one, would rather not. And I suggest you don't bother either.

The whole point and allure of a caravan is that you're taking the accommodation to the attraction. No hotel near the ancient monument you've travelled days to see? There is now. Yours.

Sadly, often petty bureaucracy will get in the way. For example, you might get arrested if your pitch is in the shadow of the Great Pyramid at Giza, Egypt. Or right outside Tutankhamun's tomb.

That said, it's surprising what you can get away with using a bit of self-confidence and determination. The young folk on the right, on a cultural tour of Europe by caravan, can't afford proper clothes or soap so certainly will be unable to pay the room bill at the Ritz Hotel. So they've done the sensible thing and pitched their caravan right under the attraction. They might be scruffy looking, but at least they've brought a small conifer to smarten up their pitch.

Out of shot is the water cannon and the 120 riot policemen.

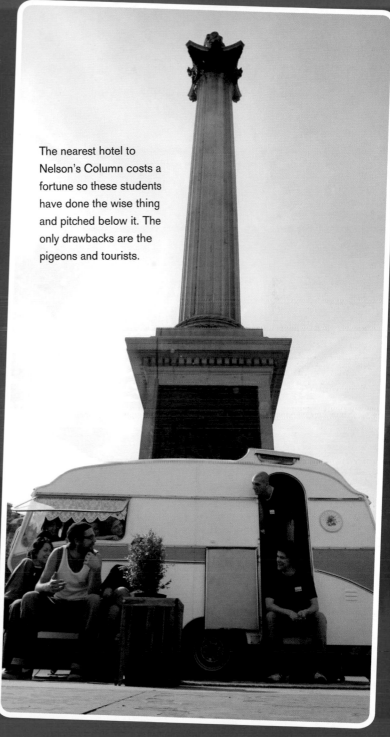

The nearest hotel to Nelson's Column costs a fortune so these students have done the wise thing and pitched below it. The only drawbacks are the pigeons and tourists.

Things to do

A caravan holiday is a wonderful way to bring the family together and bond the way families did before satellite television and PlayStation 3 were invented.

Unless the weather is dreadful and you can't go out. Now you've got a serious problem on your hands: bored children. Even with my experience of destroying caravans, I couldn't trash one as comprehensively as several small children can in a couple of rainy days. And repairing the caravan is not going to be the only expense because later there'll be days off work at Relate sessions. Since the likelihood of rain in this country is rather high it's best to be prepared.

You need games. I don't mean Monopoly, Cluedo or cards because these can make matters worse and besides, you don't have the table area. Monopoly is right out of the question because the one word you don't want mentioned on a washed-out caravan holiday is 'hotel'. So what are the alternatives? Virtually endless, limited only by your imagination. I've come up with a few suggestions for you.

Sid and Doris never go away without their solar-powered television set. It's good to get away from home for a few weeks but not at the expense of missing an episode of *Desperate Housewives* or *Strictly Ballroom Dancing Antiques.*

Caravan hide and seek. As anyone who has spent time in caravans knows, you are constantly losing things. How it is possible to mislay anything in such a small, confined space is a mystery, but that's how it is. Hide and seek can either be played with objects, such as a box of matches (always the first thing you lose when the hob doesn't have a clicky-clicky electric self-lighter), or with small people.

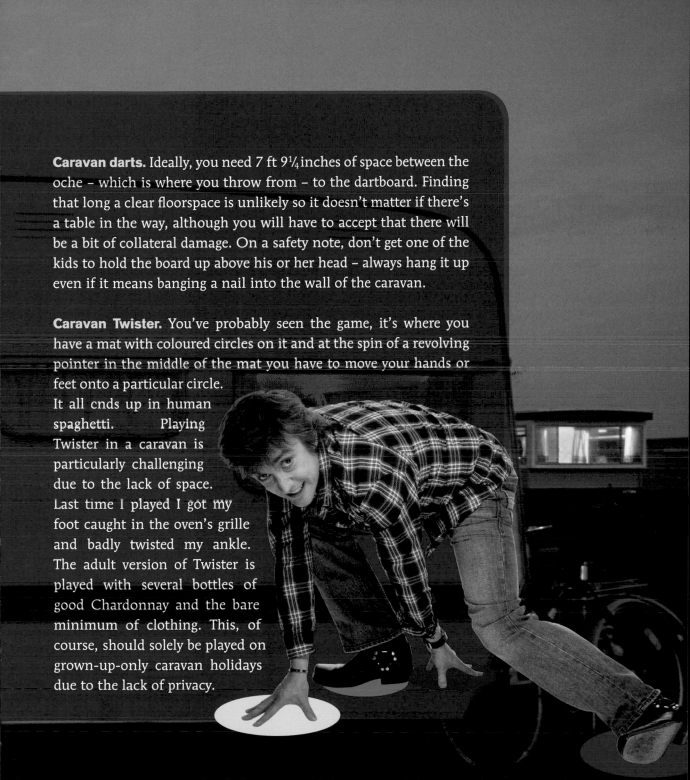

Caravan darts. Ideally, you need 7 ft 9¼ inches of space between the oche – which is where you throw from – to the dartboard. Finding that long a clear floorspace is unlikely so it doesn't matter if there's a table in the way, although you will have to accept that there will be a bit of collateral damage. On a safety note, don't get one of the kids to hold the board up above his or her head – always hang it up even if it means banging a nail into the wall of the caravan.

Caravan Twister. You've probably seen the game, it's where you have a mat with coloured circles on it and at the spin of a revolving pointer in the middle of the mat you have to move your hands or feet onto a particular circle. It all ends up in human spaghetti. Playing Twister in a caravan is particularly challenging due to the lack of space. Last time I played I got my foot caught in the oven's grille and badly twisted my ankle. The adult version of Twister is played with several bottles of good Chardonnay and the bare minimum of clothing. This, of course, should solely be played on grown-up-only caravan holidays due to the lack of privacy.

The games on the previous page will keep the family entertained, but only for a short period.

What you really need is a few furious and frantic games that will burn off energy and wipe the kids out so that you can sit back and watch the telly in peace.

Due to space restrictions and the need to have something resembling a caravan to stay in afterwards, I recommend avoiding full-contact martial arts or tag wrestling.

Idyllic isn't it? Children playing quietly outside. But it's just about to piss it down with rain and soon the angelic children will be possessed by the devil. Best have some good, hearty indoor games ready. Losers get to sleep in that tent.

British Bulldog is an excellent game and very traditional. You probably played it at a school. One member of the family is chosen as the Bulldog and the rest line up against one wall. The object is to run to the opposite wall without being 'tagged' by the Bulldog. Those who are become Bulldogs and the last person to be free is the winner. Before you start playing it's important to check that the caravan's levelling jacks are secure, otherwise the caravan will tip up. Actually, that sounds like fun because it adds a third dimension so ignore that advice.

Paintball. Just the ticket for blowing off steam on a wet holiday. A good-quality water pistol should do the job. If your caravan is in need of sprucing up then you could actually use paint. However, I'd recommend ketchup or some similar gory foodstuff. Easier to clean up afterwards.

Baked-bean dipping. This is a good one. Fill a large saucepan full of beans – at least ten cans – and then put some coins, toy cars and a few other valuables in it like your dad's Rolex watch. All the participants take a sock off and then have to fish in the beans for the goodies. After the game is finished make some toast to eat with the beans for tea. Notice the cheesy flavour to the beans.

Lastly, Spot the Difference. A player hides in the shower while you move something in the caravan. The player comes out and tries to spot what's different. A nice, non-destructive game for the end of the day.

Rules of caravan games

1) Games should involve as many family members as possible.

2) Losers have to empty the chemical loo.

3) All breakages (there will be lots) are the fault of whoever bought this book.

Draughts (below) is far too dull to play on holiday. Kids don't have the patience for it and besides, only two can play. Far better to play a more physical and violent game to keep them amused.

Small print from my lawyer: 'If any campsites or small villages are destroyed as a result of any games suggested on these pages it is not my client's fault. Anyway, he's gone to Ulan Bator and can't be contacted.'

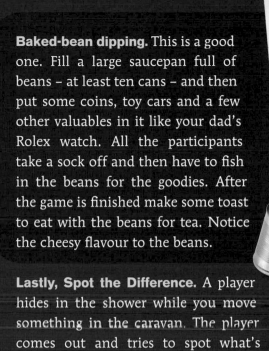

Caravan Christmas

Many think of a caravan as a summer-only residence, but why restrict the joys of living under plywood to just a few months?

One of the most rewarding things that you can do with a caravan is spend Christmas in it. Apart from the lack of chimney for Santa, there are only positive advantages to a caravan Christmas.

The major benefit is that you are very limited on space and that means the dreadful in-laws can't come for Christmas. What a shame. Fewer people means a smaller and cheaper turkey, too.

Over-the-top use of electric Santa lights can bring ridicule from neighbours, but not when there's no one around to laugh. Beware of flattening the on-board battery, though.

Now this is what Christmas used to be about. Yes, the austere years of the 1950s meant things were simpler – apparently they didn't have colour television, let alone Sky + – but simpler often means more enjoyable. This group of friends are having a very entertaining festive time by the look of it. 'Now Sidney, go easy on the Harveys Bristol Cream or you won't be able to stand for the Queen's Speech.' Cooking for the eight people in this caravan (I *can* count, one is taking the photo) would have been an enormous challenge.

Cooking

Any fool can cook in a large kitchen. It just takes a cockney accent or a lot of swearing. Cooking in a caravan, however, is a proper art. For one thing, it's incredibly easy to set fire to the kitchen because most bits of a caravan burn quite well. And that's not a problem faced by the coiffed and tended softies in the kitchens at the Ivy. There's also hardly any room for putting things down and you're lucky if you have more than a couple of gas rings. Also, it's quite likely that you forgot to buy a full gas cylinder before you went away so you might have to change the menu halfway through cooking dinner.

None of these issues should put you off because cooking is one of the greatest pleasures of caravanning. In fact, it's difficult to think of any others.

Always pack: Several boxes of matches, a tea towel for throwing over chip pan fires, a chisel for removing burned bacon from the frying pan, a mobile phone for calling Dominos pizza delivery.

The frying pan is the most important tool for the caravan chef after the shotgun. If it dies, it fries. Make use of the local fauna including rabbits, pigeons and, of course, fish, which can also be caught with a shotgun. These two ladies are flambéing a rat found behind the fold-out bed. Lovely with wild mushrooms picked on site.

Just because you're pitched in a crowded caravan park near Birmingham with children running riot outside it's no excuse to let standards drop. Always dress for dinner and make sure that your staff also keep up standards. The benefits of buying a high-roofed caravan are also obvious from the picture.

This scene of domestic bliss at the breakfast table can be dated from the classic 1970s checked-fabric curtains, the absence of MP3 Players at the table, the plastic bowls of Shredded Wheat and, of course, by daddy's classic Seventies porn star 'tache and sideburns. Mealtimes in caravans are great for bringing families together. I mean, really, really close together.

It's a trap that's easy to fall into, but don't complicate your caravan holiday by trying to recreate your garden and patio. Especially not with our climate. If it rains you'd never get this lot back inside without drowning. Yes, you can indeed cook stuff in your caravan, but really, a picnic blanket, crisps, sandwiches and Cokes is all you need for the perfect meal.

HAMMOND'S CARAVAN
Cock oh Van

1 KFC Family Feast bucket
Leftover red wine from last night
Any other alcohol dregs
Bacon bits stuck to breakfast plates
1 tin mushroom soup
Pepper
Any herbs (legal)
Pickled onions (left over from fish and chips)

Poncy food has no place in caravanning but there are occasions when you might need to show off your skills. This simple recipe is designed to impress with wonderful taste and aroma using the most simple ingredients.

Remove breadcrumbs from KFC and eat while you're cooking meal. Place everything in a large pot. Bring to the boil and open a lager. Turn down to simmer. Open another lager. Simmer for thirty minutes while drinking more lager.

At all times the chicken must be covered by wine. Open another bottle if required and have a swig for yourself. Congratulations, this fabulous dish is ready be eaten by your lucky guests.

I need to go

It's extremely important on a caravan holiday to avoid using the on-board toilet at all costs because they're really gross.

Ideally, you want to stay on a caravan site with a brand new toilet block with doors that lock properly, humorous graffiti and an endless supply of soft toilet paper. Unfortunately this is not always possible and eventually you will have to use the smallest room. A visit to the loo in a caravan is fraught with problems. Firstly, caravans have paper-thin walls so every fart and toilet 'sound effect' will be heard by everyone. Most off-putting. Second, because the room is ridiculously small you can't read a newspaper on the potty and will have to read a mini-dictionary of Serbo-Croat instead.

This is a prototype of an early Portaloo. It never caught on because of several accidents during trials when the truck moved off while someone was still on the throne, causing serious injury and great embarrassment.

Dr Who's Tardis looks really small on the outside but open the door and it's bigger than an Airbus hangar. A caravan toilet looks really small but when you open the door it's even smaller inside. It's against the law to keep a gerbil in a space that small.

Ready for some potty science? Chemical loos used to be filled with formaldehyde — the stuff they preserve dead bodies with — but it irritates the skin and nose so today stuff called glutaraldehyde and quaternary ammonium compounds is used. Impressed? Don't be, I looked it up on Wikipedia.

There's only one thing worse than having to use the loo in a caravan and that's having to empty it. Actually there is another, and that's using a loo that should have been emptied but hasn't. Ugh.

If everyone had a vindaloo last night and there's no facility other than the caravan's bog, then dig your own loo. Dig down about 10 inches and the rest is obvious.

Accessories

I can't stand those programmes on telly when some bloke in a daft shirt wafts into your living room and takes the mickey out of your sofas.

It's all too easy to get carried away with 'interior design' and forget that all you need is a flat surface to stand your dinner on, a cupboard for spare pants and a comfy chair to watch the telly from. Fortunately the style 'guru' has historically overlooked the interior of the caravan leaving it unsullied by 'ragroll' paint effects and contemporary soft furnishings. Meaning that the caravan interior is a true reflection of the taste of its occupants and not put there by the insistence of some visiting dandy with frilly cuffs and a TV crew. They are an historic document. And are mostly tartan.

Your caravan will look this smart for about a day after you've bought it. Once the family has been in it it's downhill until I come in and destroy it with a gallon of super unleaded.

This is what happens when you get too clever with organisation and design. Extremely neat and tidy but at the expense of living accommodation. This caravan would suit someone who'd spent most of his or her life down a coal mine or in a similarly cramped environment.

If a style expert comes into your caravan and questions your use of 1970s brothel leather cushions with striped velour throw him or her out immediately. A caravan is your personal space and should be respected as such regardless of furnishing materials.

Must haves

Packing for a holiday is pretty straightforward. Passport, tickets, toothbrush, suncream and a spare pair of undies (more than one if you're female).

Straightforward if you're going on a package holiday but for a caravanning holiday assembling a kit list is far more complicated. You're essentially taking your house with you. Most of the things that you'll need are pretty obvious. Like loo paper (at least 20 rolls), but there are other important items that you should take with you. There are many helpful websites run by motoring organisations that list them in great detail but nonetheless I find that often things are left off. Like explosives. I've put together a shortlist of essentials that I would not dream of leaving home without.

Noise is the ruin of a good caravan holiday. Usually it comes from your own children. Plonk a pair of these ear defenders on your noggin and you'll have peace.

The electric click-click thingy that lights the gas hob will rarely work so you'll be needing plenty of matches. Can be used as a currency with fellow campers. Like fags in a prison.

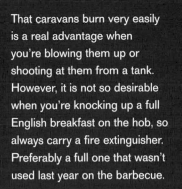

That caravans burn very easily is a real advantage when you're blowing them up or shooting at them from a tank. However, it is not so desirable when you're knocking up a full English breakfast on the hob, so always carry a fire extinguisher. Preferably a full one that wasn't used last year on the barbecue.

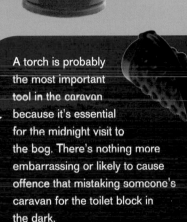

A torch is probably the most important tool in the caravan because it's essential for the midnight visit to the bog. There's nothing more embarrassing or likely to cause offence that mistaking someone's caravan for the toilet block in the dark.

A hand grenade is an extremely useful tool. If the best pitch is already taken an accurately chucked grenade will quickly clear it. Also useful for unblocking chemical toilets (never sit on it while clearing it) and getting apples down from branches that you can't reach.

How to be a good caravanner

Caravan etiquette is a key part of life on the road. It's important to behave correctly whether you're on holiday in a caravan, selling saveloys from one or placing a retired caravan in the sights of your anti-tank rifle.

In the latter case it's extremely impolite to blow up a caravan before checking that its owner has finished with it. Especially if the owner is sleeping inside at the time.

Many people have a downer on the caravan, usually because they're stuck behind one on their way to an overpriced hotel with cockroaches in the bathroom. They're just jealous. When they overtake you shouting abuse, don't make rude signs at them. Get the kids to do it instead as it'll annoy them even more.

World peace and kindness to all caravanners is easy if you just follow some simple guidelines. I've laid down Hammond's caravanning commandments on the page opposite.

Ye Caravan Commandments

☞ Thou shalt not play loudly at night heavy metal or anything by Boyzone.

☞ Thou shalt not allow pet dobermann to eat other caravanners or crapeth on their pitches.

☞ If thou eateth a chicken vindaloo with a gassy beer thou must kippeth outside.

☞ Thou must not empty thine chemical loo out onto another's pitch or into the water supply.

☞ Thou must not practise folk dancing in daylight.

☞ Thou shalt not steal gas bottles. Unless it's really cold and yours is empty.

☞ Thou shalt not hang wind chimes.

☞ Thou shalt not hang old pants from the washing line.

By order
Lord Hammond

4 Homes on Wheels

The caravan is the most versatile machine ever invented. There are no limits to what you can use a caravan for. You can holiday in it, live full time in it, sell stuff from it and use it as an intercontinental ballistic missile.

In this chapter your eyes will be opened to a world of caravanning that you don't see on the M3 motorway on an August bank holiday or read about in *Practical Caravan* magazine. We'll be meeting priests and politicians, eccentrics and old ladies who can tell you who you're going to marry and the winner of the 3.30 handicap race at Haydock Park.

We've already looked at games that you can play in caravans, now we're going to deal with games that you can play with a caravan. Naturally, explosives, demolition and danger are all involved. If you don't have my destructive streak, we'll show you what you can do with your caravan when it's finally unfit for human habitation (which it has been for most of its life, to be honest).

Static homes

When I see acres of fields full of static caravans two words come to my mind: 'Eurofighter' and 'missile'. Sorry, but they're too ugly to be allowed to live.

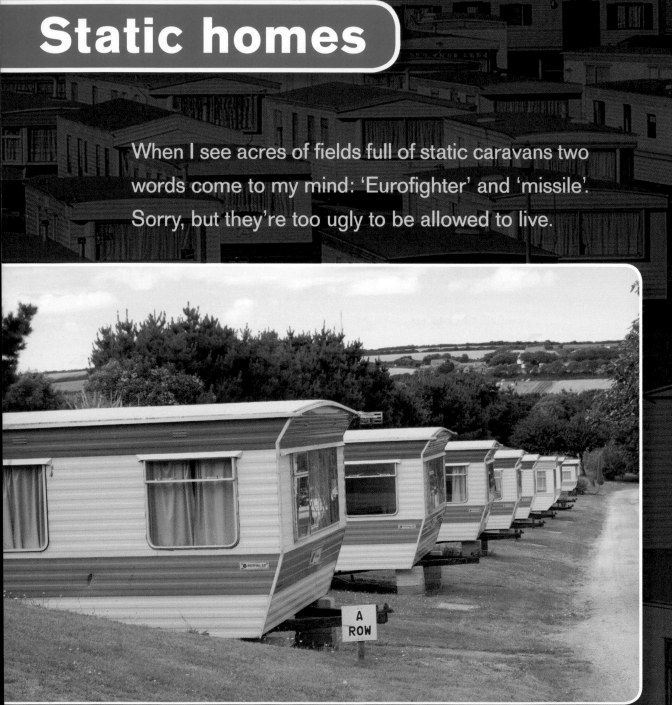

A ROW

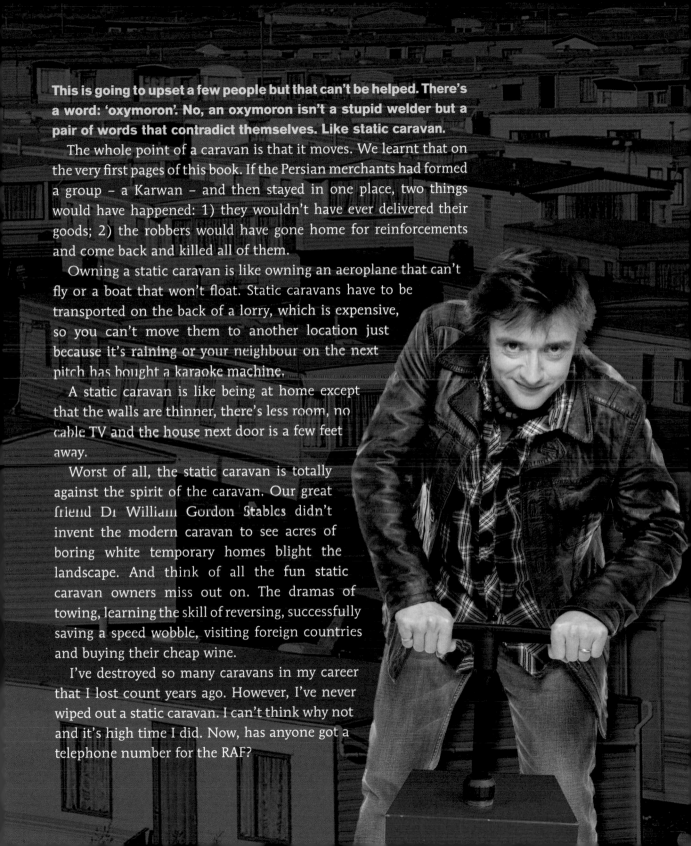

This is going to upset a few people but that can't be helped. There's a word: 'oxymoron'. No, an oxymoron isn't a stupid welder but a pair of words that contradict themselves. Like static caravan.

The whole point of a caravan is that it moves. We learnt that on the very first pages of this book. If the Persian merchants had formed a group – a Karwan – and then stayed in one place, two things would have happened: 1) they wouldn't have ever delivered their goods; 2) the robbers would have gone home for reinforcements and come back and killed all of them.

Owning a static caravan is like owning an aeroplane that can't fly or a boat that won't float. Static caravans have to be transported on the back of a lorry, which is expensive, so you can't move them to another location just because it's raining or your neighbour on the next pitch has bought a karaoke machine.

A static caravan is like being at home except that the walls are thinner, there's less room, no cable TV and the house next door is a few feet away.

Worst of all, the static caravan is totally against the spirit of the caravan. Our great friend Dr William Gordon Stables didn't invent the modern caravan to see acres of boring white temporary homes blight the landscape. And think of all the fun static caravan owners miss out on. The dramas of towing, learning the skill of reversing, successfully saving a speed wobble, visiting foreign countries and buying their cheap wine.

I've destroyed so many caravans in my career that I lost count years ago. However, I've never wiped out a static caravan. I can't think why not and it's high time I did. Now, has anyone got a telephone number for the RAF?

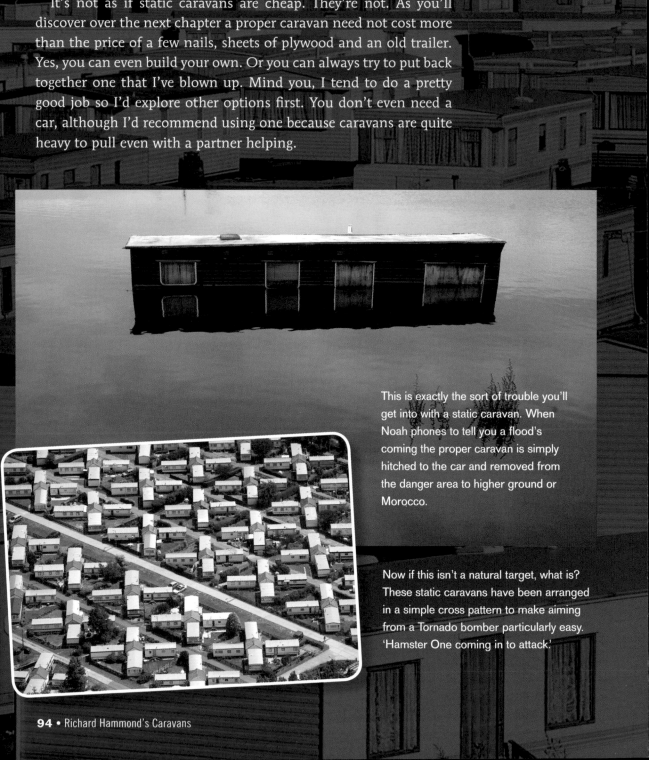

It's not as if static caravans are cheap. They're not. As you'll discover over the next chapter a proper caravan need not cost more than the price of a few nails, sheets of plywood and an old trailer. Yes, you can even build your own. Or you can always try to put back together one that I've blown up. Mind you, I tend to do a pretty good job so I'd explore other options first. You don't even need a car, although I'd recommend using one because caravans are quite heavy to pull even with a partner helping.

This is exactly the sort of trouble you'll get into with a static caravan. When Noah phones to tell you a flood's coming the proper caravan is simply hitched to the car and removed from the danger area to higher ground or Morocco.

Now if this isn't a natural target, what is? These static caravans have been arranged in a simple cross pattern to make aiming from a Tornado bomber particularly easy. 'Hamster One coming in to attack.'

Trailer tents

While I have a strong desire to scramble fighter jets to attack static caravans, I am much calmer about trailer tents.

Even though I dislike them a lot. They're bought by people who are a bit confused because they're not sure what hobby they want to practise. Tents and caravans are different, don't try to combine them.

This trailer tent's design (above) was influenced by the Apollo Lunar Module but that doesn't make it any less useless or unattractive.

The trailer tent combines the worst of both worlds. As this photo shows (left) you get all the leaks, pneumonia, draughts and insects of camping with the added hassle of having to tow the tent. A tent goes on your back when you've slept in it, not on the back of your car.

Virtual caravan

This simple shed conversion will give you most of the sensations of life in a caravan: shortage of space, spiders, cold, being unable to sleep when it's raining hard and the smell of wet wood.

Creating a small garden is acceptable but avoid an excessive gnome population or model windmills.

For extra caravan realism install the most basic sanitation system possible. This bucket will do nicely. Yuk.

The home virtual caravan will make perfect accommodation for annoying relatives or as a punishment block for poorly behaved children.

The inability to drive a car – whether for health, legal or religious reasons – or the lack of a car for whatever reason doesn't mean that you have to miss out on all the pleasures of caravanning because today we live in a virtual world where anything is possible.

You don't need the CGI skills of a top Hollywood studio to go virtual caravanning. All you need is some plywood, nails, glue and a few simple tools like a chainsaw, a big hammer and your next door neighbour's old kitchen units. And, of course, a good imagination. A virtual caravan in the garden is obviously not as good as the real thing due to the rather predictable scenery, but at least you can pop into the house and have a decent shower and use a proper loo.

This virtual caravan was built by a prominent member of the green movement who gave up caravanning for ecological reasons. For minimum impact on the environment its owner has painted the caravan to blend in with the stone wall behind it. A karma chameleon van.

Motorhomes

Motorhomes used to be called motor caravans. I don't know why the name was changed. Perhaps people with motor caravans saw the lavish mobile palaces used by Hollywood A-listers and thought that if they called their Ford Transit motor caravan a 'motorhome' people would think that Angelina Jolie once got dressed in it.

As many of you will have noticed, I rather like cars. You'd think that if I love cars and engines I would much prefer something with an engine than without. Like a food mixer powered by a Honda Fireblade motorbike engine. Or a caravan with an engine. But no, I still prefer the engineless caravan. Why?

Well for one thing they are much easier to destroy and crash cars through. Apart from items like cookers, most parts of an old caravan will fall to bits with a large sneeze and certainly a flying Lada. Motorhomes contain hard items like engines and gearboxes that don't crumple when you hit them.

The other problem with motorhomes is that they're not very practical. Parking is a nightmare. What happens if you have to nip into a town to buy something important (like my book)? Ah, says the motorhome fanatic, 'You tow a small car or attach a scooter to the back of it.' Er right, that makes sense. Caravanners are more sensible. They attach the car to the front and tow the home.

An early prototype motorhome undergoing secret testing somewhere poor. As with prototype cars, initial testing is often done with 'mules' — vehicles that are not the finished product but use the mechanical bits underneath a dummy body. This one is very unfinished and is being towed by mules.

Unfortunately, Ford's Transit-based accordion failed to take the market by storm.

The good news is that it inspired someone to come up with the idea of an extendable roof. Not particularly necessary in my case, but many people find vans short on headroom.

Status Quo and many other rock bands started their careers travelling around in Ford Transit vans just like this one.

This is an early motorhome using the Ford Transit chassis. A simple device that is essentially a pick-up truck and a small caravan brought together with a few bolts and a cheap set of spanners. The bit over the cab is called the 'Luton'. Like a 'futon', it's an uncomfortable place to sleep.

After Herbert Smyth's wife Sybil left him for a man with a proper car, Herbert toured the country on his Vespa motor scooter combination with his beloved pet terrier Trumper riding in the side kennel. Unfortunately, Trumper also left, fed up with the appalling ride comfort offered by the scooter's tiny wheels.

One of the advantages of the motorhome is that it is so easy to build. This one has been built out of an army surplus vehicle and looks very tough. Not the sort of thing I would risk jumping a car through. Looks like it might be rather tricky to blow up, too.

Modern cars very rarely break down, but post-war models like this Austin were very unreliable. Turning one into living accommodation, albeit very basic, provided owners with somewhere to live while waiting for the rescue services to turn up. It's not big enough to be any use for a proper holiday. Unless you're short, single and friendless.

Formula One experts are always going on about how much engineering and high tech thinking goes into their racing cars. It's true, but that's nothing compared to the amount of effort that goes into designing the drivers' motorhomes.

Coming last in the race is nothing like as embarrassing as your fellow drivers discovering that you spent less than a million quid on your motorhome and that it has only two loos and one sauna.

F1 star Jenson Button poses alongside his modest motorhome. Button uses his home for 'entertaining' at the races but of course, never drives the thing himself. He'll have a private jet for travelling distances of over 2 miles. And a helicopter. And a yacht.

The monster motorhomes that blokes like Button and his mates play with are almost all built in America. That's why they're so big. There are only three trees in Texas and no sharp corners. Guiding something the size of a small village is straightforward when the roads are straight and wide enough to land the new Airbus A380 on. Sideways. But take one of these massive moving hotels onto our quaint and rustic country lanes and pretty soon you'll be wedged between walls or have knocked bits off it.

The only place where driving an American motorhome is easy in the UK is on motorways, and do you really want to spend a holiday going up and down the M6? I thought not.

I'm pretty sure that a lot of people who own big yank motorhomes are frustrated truck drivers. Like those people who drive their breakdown trucks with the yellow lights flashing even though they've only got a broken Metro on the back – they want to be firemen. Surely it would be much easier to write to Eddie Stobart for a job?

That's enough of motorhomes or motor caravans. Bring me one to blow up, but otherwise I'll stick to the simple world of TNT and caravans. I suggest you do the same. Well, perhaps not the TNT.

Only in America. Yet another ridiculous idea that wouldn't work in Britain. 'Now listen here, buddy, there are these things called hotels, and these hotels have things called rooms, bars and swimming pools, and you can stay in them. And they can't be jack-knifed.

Oddest

I've never blown up or destroyed the same caravan twice (I mean of the same type, because obviously once you've blown one up there's nothing left to blow up again). That's not just professional pride talking, caravans come in so many shapes and sizes that there are so many to choose from.

From the over-the-top world of 'I'm a celebrity get me a motorhome' we're back to the down-to-earth world of the caravan. Thank God for that. Over the next couple of pages you'll see a splendid selection of different styles of caravan. You may laugh at some, but each one suits its owner just perfectly and is a source of much pride. Mind you, the poodle caravan (below) takes a bit of understanding.

Earning a penny

Finding a clean and sanitary public toilet in busy towns is often next to impossible. Here inventor Bert Thrapplewhite demonstrates his ingenious solution to the problem of spending a penny in the city. It's his patent 'carava n khazi'. Bert went on to make a fortune from his porta-potty, often parking it outside places like pubs and Indian restaurants where the queues for in-house facilities are often long and unpleasant.

Zero emissions

Olympic cyclist Henk Podlomoistor out training for a long-distance event. A committed green campaigner, Henk often hitches his racing bike to this vintage caravan to combine training with a short touring holiday. The caravan contains a full high-tech gym and exercise pool, plus accommodation for Henk's travelling physiotherapist.

Caravan karma

What does your caravan say about you? The sight of me standing in front of a pile of burning plywood and charred kitchen units with a still smoking rocket-propelled grenade launcher in my arms obviously hints at some sort of issue from my childhood.

Other less destructive people express their beliefs about life through their caravans. Whatever their persuasion, passion or eccentricity, caravanners don't give a toss about what other people think. It's not that they're life's rebels, it's more to do with spending years being honked at by angry people in Ford Mondeos who have no patience or understanding of the importance of towing a caravan slowly across the Severn Bridge when there's a force 8 gale blowing.

For some the caravan is a castle. Sir Reginald Fanshawe bt, MC, KFC, B&Q retired, poses beside his Lee Enfield Shooter, sword raised ready to fend off any attackers. Or saboteurs hell bent on disconnecting his 240v power hook-up.

Some people will go to enormous lengths to avoid the people from the TV licensing department. This rustic caravan arrangement on the edge of a forest doubles as a second-hand clothes shop. Business is unlikely to be brisk as it's a bit off the main high street.

Some caravanners are like that bald bloke on the *Kung Fu* TV series who travelled the world seeking enlightenment or the answer to the 'Big Question'. That you can discover the meaning of life living in a forest in a rotting thirty-year-old Explorer Eureka 25 is debatable, but I'm glad there are people who try.

Stamp your own personality on your caravan by decorating its outside with treasured artefacts. This caravan is obviously owned by someone in the cooking or chemistry business.

Working from home

For many people a caravan is more than a holiday home on wheels. It's a premises. Yes, the caravan is the perfect place from which to run a business. So perfect, I'm surprised they're not used more often.

You don't need to have been on *Dragon's Den* to understand why the caravan makes such a good business premises. I've never bought a shop, but I'd imagine that there's a lot of paperwork and solicitors involved, both of which are worth avoiding. Buying a caravan is easy. The beauty of a caravan is that you can move it easily to a new location. Not easy to do with a large supermarket. Caravans are also pretty cheap, especially if you don't need a very smart one for your business.

So if your business is selling umbrellas and it stops raining where you are, or worse, there's a drought, you simply telephone the Met Office and ask them where it's raining. Bingo, you're back in business. Then there's the ability to swiftly move on if the £149.50 laptop computers that you've been selling don't actually contain any software. Or batteries. Or electronics.

Is this the world's smallest cinema? A brilliant idea. Oi, don't drop popcorn on the upholstery, please.

The somewhat daunting-looking Madam Smith is apparently the famous Madam Smith from Yorkshire TV. Being able to up sticks quickly is very important for fortune-tellers in case what they foretell turns out to be complete bollocks.

The rather more upmarket facility used by the 'Original Gypsy Rose Lee'. Actually, the original Gypsy Rose Lee was a stripper who died in 1970. You can claim anything if you won't be around tomorrow.

Of course, one of the greatest contributions the caravan makes is in the field (often literally) of mobile catering. Apart from being a passionate caravan exterminator, I'm also into motorbikes in a big way. Trouble with bikes is that you get cold on them in winter and in summer your bum gets sore from being in the saddle all day. Either way, you're always looking for a place to recover.

And that place is often a roadside eatery that in a previous life was a touring caravan. Every time I blow up a caravan I have one nagging thought: 'I hope this caravan wasn't going to be a greasy spoon.' You can't beat a mug of tea and a piping hot bacon sarnie dripping with lard served by the smiling owner of a roadside caravan café. The best establishments provide plastic seating and an awning for customers. Many of these places deserve a Michelin star as much as any poncy restaurant.

'Excuse me miss, can you direct me to the nearest branch of Game Zone?'

The wheels of democracy

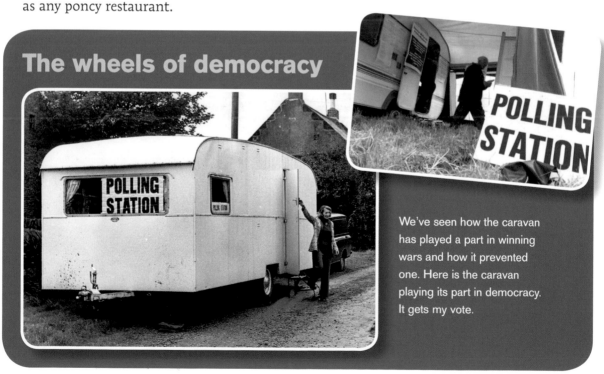

We've seen how the caravan has played a part in winning wars and how it prevented one. Here is the caravan playing its part in democracy. It gets my vote.

Law and order

Big Brother (the real one, not the telly programme) has made great use of the caravan in keeping the seething masses under control. There's something daunting about a caravan with 'police' written on the side. I've always wondered, do they have cells in them?

Don't think Inspector Morse would think much of this nick on wheels. It looks a right mess and might not even be road legal.

This old caravan is serving as customs post somewhere near the Mexican border in the US. Note how boards have been placed around the bottom to stop illegal immigrants from hiding underneath it.

From cradle...

Most of us have caravan memories from childhood. Holidays spent fighting with siblings and rain. Unfortunately, I came late to the world of caravans (but when I did I entered with a bang), but that doesn't mean that caravans didn't have a place in the Hammond family album. I bought candyfloss from them, went to them for first aid when the big boys picked on me at the local fun fair and chased girls into them when I was a rugged and highly fancied teenager. Actually, I made that up. Not the candyfloss bit. Or the part about being beaten up.

After three weeks still no one had come to claim the three Snott children from the campsite's Lost Children Centre. The one on the right is now a top judge, the middle one is senior partner in a merchant bank and the one on the left is a celebrity chef.

These schoolkids have just had a philosophy lesson in the temporary classroom behind them. Fortunately, the one without glasses has chemistry next and is planning to blow up the caravan. Good lad.

To...

The lord moves in mysterious ways . . . sometimes in a caravan. If the flock won't come to church, then take the church to the flock. If you can sell kebabs from a caravan then why not the word of God?

Most ecclesiastical caravans are conversions, but surely there's a market for purpose-built models. How about the Webley Second Coming or the Bethlehem Manger 45?

This splendid combination of classic vehicles is just the ticket for missionary work. The group later changed its name to the 'Caravangelists' for obvious reasons.

By the sombre expressions it looks like a funeral is being conducted. What a way to go. But surely a caravan is better suited to getting hitched? Saves having to ask too many relations to the ceremony and blowing loads of cash on champagne.

Games with caravans

This is one of the reasons that I and so many thousands of others love them: there's so much you can do with caravans and you're only limited by your own imagination.

I've had loads of fun over the years inventing caravan games. Or more specifically, taking family favourites and substituting caravans. The wonderful thing about caravans is that when they're old and stink so badly that a tramp wouldn't go near them, they're worth almost nothing. And so can be picked up for a song. Often, people are glad to be rid of the things, thus missing out on perhaps the most interesting and exciting chapter in a caravan's life: the end.

Every schoolboy loves a game of conkers, so grown-up boys (and girls) will love my **caravan conker** game. All you need is two old caravans and two large cranes. It may not sound entirely practical, but renting cranes is easy and it doesn't take long to get the hang of working them. You do get through caravans quite quickly so make sure you bring at least half a dozen.

Much safer than traditional conkers and no one can cheat by soaking a caravan in vinegar and baking it in an oven to make it harder. These two caravans will soon be piles of plywood on the ground and one of the chaps the happy winner of caravan conkers.

Caravan darts is another great game that you can play, although setting this one up is a little complicated and requires some DIY skills. If you've ever moved a caravan around you'll know they're quite heavy, so unless you've got a bionic arm you'll need to make a device for throwing a caravan.

Fortunately people in medieval times designed something called a trebuchet, which is like a giant catapult. Once you've made your throwing machine you simply mark out a target, put on a shiny shirt and some gold jewellery and you're ready for a game of caravan darts.

The possibilities are endless. Next time a large river floods nip along with a couple of dead caravans for a game of **pooh sticks**. Obviously, low bridges have to be avoided.

How about **caravan skittles**? An easy one, this one. All you need to do is rig up a hitch that can be undone from inside the car. Then make some skittles – two plastic dustbins glued end-to-end would do. To play, drive at the skittles, releasing the caravan at the right moment so that it veers away to hit them and score a strike, impressing your friends. Best played in a field. Or someone else's garden.

Outdoor activities have never been more popular. Or rather, the image of outdoor sports has never been. If everyone who bought an item of surf clothing actually went surfing the ferries would have to stop running because there wouldn't be any room on the sea for them.

The ruggard outdoorsmen who can live for months on damp leaves and squirrel droppings are probably very rude about caravans. I'm only guessing they are because the last thing I would want to do is hang around with blokes with beards who dig their own toilets. Anyway, we can get involved in these macho rugged activities even if we don't all own No Fear tee-shirts because there are many hairy chested sports for which the caravan is perfectly suited.

White water rafting. Any fool can shoot a raging torrent in a purpose-built and very buoyant rubber dinghy but it takes enormous bravery and not a small measure of rash lunacy to launch oneself down a canyon full of boiling white water in a caravan. Because it is made from plywood a caravan will actually float, just not for very long. And not for very long at all if you hit a larger boulder with it.

Then there's **caravan skydiving**. This is not easy to organise but there was an advertisement in which a car was thrown out of the back of a transport aeroplane so it must be possible. Obviously it is not a good idea to be in the caravan when it is free-falling and an even worse one to be in it when it hits the ground. Perhaps a good compromise would be to go down halfway inside it and at the crucial moment leap out of the door and open your parachute. This way you will be sure to land fairly near it and be able to see it explode as it hits the ground. It's a sight I'd love to see.

I once crossed the English Channel in a car. Or rather, I tried to. A caravan would have been a wiser choice, perhaps using a sail made out of sheets. Due to the large amount of airspace and the natural buoyancy of plywood the craft should float quite well. But then I thought that about the car, too.

Caravan RIP

Recycling is a great invention. People in a few centuries' time will look back and marvel that we, as a society, were happy to get rid of our waste by burying it in the ground where it lies for thousands of years, killing moles and refusing to do the decent thing and disappear. They might also be quite surprised that we willingly confined ourselves to small plastic boxes to suffer one another's bodily odours and share a bucket to wee in. And called it a holiday. But then, hey, what do people of the future know anyway? They should have been here…

Obviously, as the saviour of humankind and the source of countless thousands of hours of unalloyed if slightly cramped joy, it's only right that the caravan should be at the very forefront of the recycling revolution. Because the caravan is one household item that really can be recycled when it's finished with. It's hard to think of, I know, but there comes a time when your Diamond Intercontinental Naturist 25 is unfit for human habitation. It must be retired. You've bought the new Naturist 32 but that's no reason to chuck the old one away because there's bound to be a use for it. It's the equivalent of a noble and proud racehorse being put out to pasture, perhaps to sire a new generation in its own, glorious image. Only this is a caravan, so without the sex. And the glorious stuff. Or the nobility.

'Hey, watch what you're doing with that chainsaw, there's years of life left in that caravan.' How about turning it into a **tree house**. How ironic would that be? All you need is some strong rope and a gang of able-bodied men to hoist it into the boughs of a stout tree.

Garden sheds cost a packet. And that's not the end of it because if you buy a cheapo one from a DIY store you're expected to erect the thing yourself. And persuading things that come flat-packed to be anything other than flat and packed is difficult and undignified. There's another problem with

sheds: you can't move them once they're up. This simple caravan-shed was made in 20 minutes using an axe and two door hinges. There's plenty of room in there for that old plastic sledge, a pile of plastic plant pots, a rusty old saw, a box of records and a fleet of spiders bigger than badgers. Everything you need, in fact, in a shed.

We've only scratched the surface with these illustrated suggestions. The are dozens of other possibilities. Ever wanted a sauna room but haven't got room in the house for it? No problem, turn your dead caravan into one. Can't be difficult, all you need is about four kettles and a wooden bench. Fancied one of those 'meditation rooms' you read about in designer magazines? An old caravan, a couple of tea lights, a poster of Jim Morrison and a beanbag and Bob's your uncle, you'll be transcendental in seconds. A 'Love Dungeon' like the one I read about once in a magazine somewhere? Easy: one caravan, a wooden bench, a pair of handcuffs and a length of rubber hosing and 'oooh nurse, the screens'. There you go.

Horses are lovely animals and great fun. The trouble is if you keep them in the house they wreck everything. The alternative is a **stable** but these are extremely expensive as they're often attached to castles. The solution is to make Dobbin a nice house out of your old caravan. It'll be warm and dry in winter and you can even leave the telly in there to keep him or her entertained. And it will smell better than it did after two weeks in Devon with the family in it.

Practically every part of a caravan can be recycled. It was bio-degradable before anyone ever thought of recycling banks and re-using carrier bags. In fact, from the day you buy it your caravan is trying to recycle itself, especially if you leave wet clothes behind wardrobes that encourage delamination (see jargon section).

The most useful part of the dead caravan is a the metal chassis. You might not have seen this bit of your caravan before but it's the bit that the whole thing sits on. Removed from the caravan it'll make the basis of a great car or motorcyle trailer. Or you could even use it to make one of those floats that you see driving through idyllic villages during country fairs.

Keen birdwatchers use something called a hide. A hide is a structure from which you can observe birds without them realising that you're doing so.

A dead caravan (above) makes a perfect hide because the birds will confuse you for lost holiday makers.

With luck you might be able to derive a small income from your dead caravan. Luck, in that you might find someone so desperate that they'll ignore the vile smells and leaky roof. How about renting it out as a small office? Many businesses only need a table and a telephone – such as a mini-cab office. In many towns office space is extremely expensive so it won't be difficult to undercut estate agents. You might just have to lie a bit about the facilities. Wireless network? Absolutely (of course it's wireless, it doesn't even have electricity). Does it comply with office space Health and Safety regulations? Naturally (in Albania).

Loads of us fantasise about getting away from it all to a remote place where you can't hear traffic and the TV licence inspector will never catch up with you. Perhaps to a log cabin with a roaring fire set in a pine forest and surrounded by snow-capped peaks.

It's called the Grizzly Adams syndrome and is easily cured if you live in Canada or northern Scandinavia. However, log cabins are rather rare in Macclesfield. This is no problem if you have a deceased caravan to hand.

It's simple, just before your caravan has completely had it tow it to the nearest forest and leave it. Presto, you now have your own forest retreat.

Now all you have to do is put a table and chair in it, some candles and a bottle of whisky and within months you will have knocked out a best-selling novel. It's as easy as that. For an even more authentic look you can paint the caravan green or brown and grow stuff around it so that it blends in with nature. You will too after months without running water.

If you are driven mad being stuck behind caravans
we've got bad news for you: you ain't
seen nothing yet because
one day everyone will
own one.

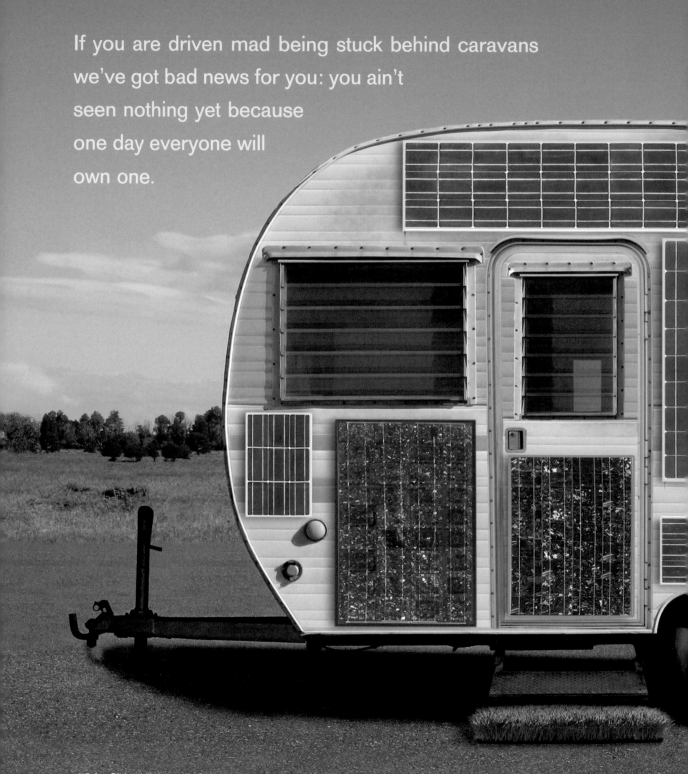

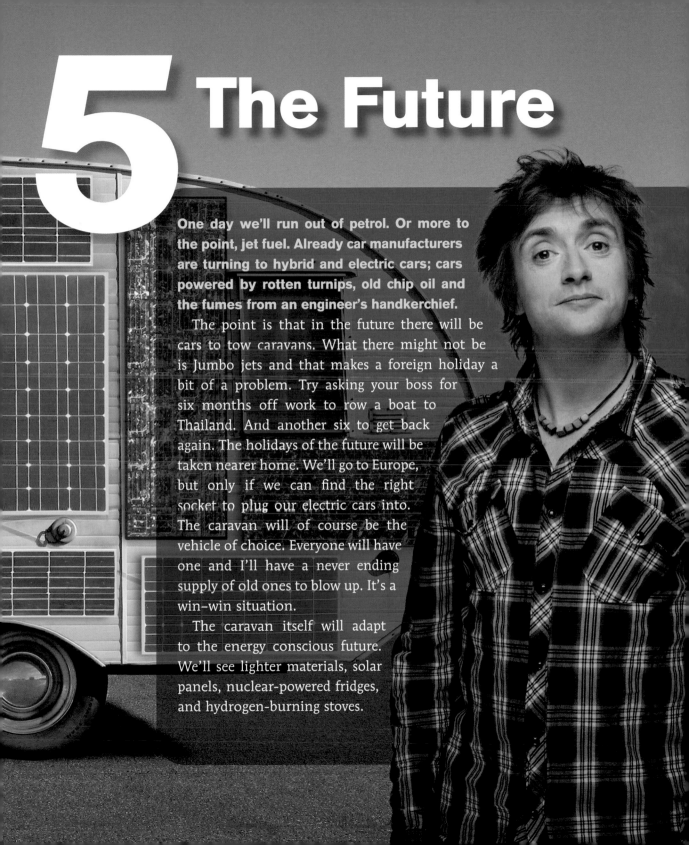

5 The Future

One day we'll run out of petrol. Or more to the point, jet fuel. Already car manufacturers are turning to hybrid and electric cars; cars powered by rotten turnips, old chip oil and the fumes from an engineer's handkerchief.

The point is that in the future there will be cars to tow caravans. What there might not be is Jumbo jets and that makes a foreign holiday a bit of a problem. Try asking your boss for six months off work to row a boat to Thailand. And another six to get back again. The holidays of the future will be taken nearer home. We'll go to Europe, but only if we can find the right socket to plug our electric cars into. The caravan will of course be the vehicle of choice. Everyone will have one and I'll have a never ending supply of old ones to blow up. It's a win–win situation.

The caravan itself will adapt to the energy conscious future. We'll see lighter materials, solar panels, nuclear-powered fridges, and hydrogen-burning stoves.

Build your own

It might be responsible for saving the world and inspiring generations of nomadic seekers of solitude, but the caravan is an incredibly simple structure. And while therein, perhaps, lies the secret of its mystical magic and its grip on the human soul, it's possible to think of it also as being no more than a floor, four walls and a roof. And a pair or two of wheels. You can use pretty much any material you have lying around to make your own, but plywood is the most traditional so grab a hammer and a mouthful of nails and get building: you'll not only save a fortune but you will finish up with a caravan that is exactly to your specification. They make suits to fit people exactly, and coffins. So why not tailor your own caravan?

These newlyweds have wisely enlisted the help of the bride's parents in building their first home. In Amish communities in America it's a tradition that everyone helps build newlyweds their first house. A wonderful idea, but building land is expensive in Europe so a caravan is the best this family can do.

This splendid home-built caravan is based on a trailer tent. Unfortunately the trailer tent's owner, a retired basketball player, found that it was seriously lacking in roof height. Being a practical fellow, albeit a bit short of funds, he set to with a pile of second-hand plywood and an old door. The result is this custom 'Hi Boy' caravan. High-speed towing would not be recommended and his car's fuel consumption will be appalling due to the enormous frontal area, but otherwise it's a job well done and one to be proud of.

I'm not quite sure of the purpose of this sturdy-looking home-built. It could be a row of outside loos, an office or transportable greyhound kennels. Whatever, its solid construction will have given its owner many years of valuable service and will continue to do so. It looks as though it might have spent its early life as a train carriage. Hard to find on eBay, but if you can pick up an old piece of rolling stock it does make a fantastic starting point for a home-built caravan. Once you've got all the graffiti and chewing gum off its insides, that is.

Customising

As more and more people take to caravanning, more young and arty people will start to buy them. And when you put art and youth together, you get customising.

Sadly the caravan has been seriously neglected by the customising industry. It's a shame because the caravan needs an injection of character. I do my bit by turning them into brightly coloured fireballs but, generally speaking, all caravans are boringly white. And predicably square in shape. This last bit might change in the future due to the need to reduce fuel consumption. A shape less like a brick loo – or a caravan – would save energy. Look at the gorgeous aluminium streamliner below. Lovely. But there's a problem: does the shape remind you of anything? An aeroplane wing perhaps? Exactly. Tow this baby up to a decent speed and you'll go from driver to pilot to dead person in seconds. Actually, all you'd need to do is tow it from the other end and then it would glide through the air and cling to the road like a Formula One car or a piece of chewing gum.

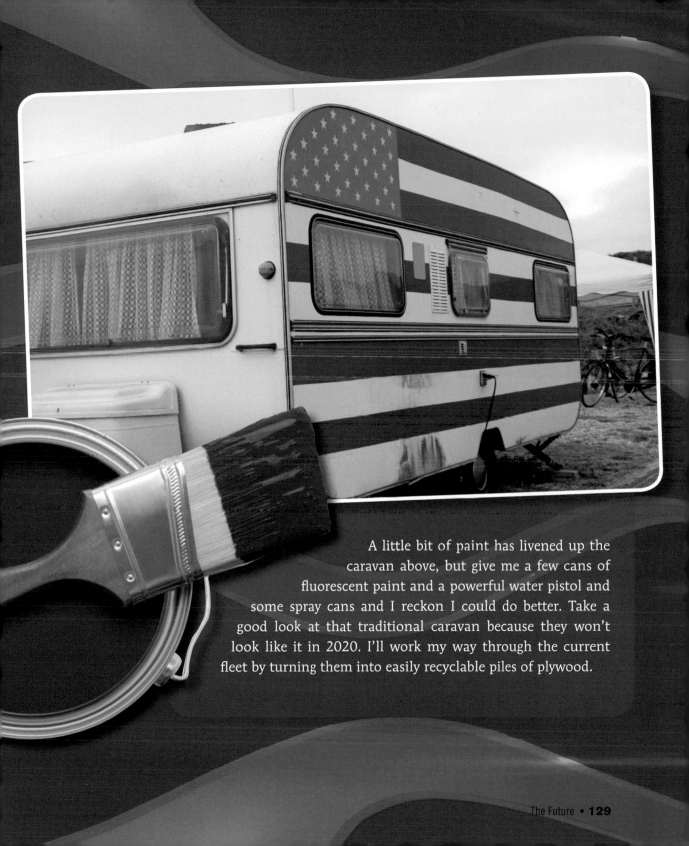

A little bit of paint has livened up the caravan above, but give me a few cans of fluorescent paint and a powerful water pistol and some spray cans and I reckon I could do better. Take a good look at that traditional caravan because they won't look like it in 2020. I'll work my way through the current fleet by turning them into easily recyclable piles of plywood.

'Send around four dozen oysters, a Cornish lobster and six bottles of Moët & Chandon. Oh, and two Calor gas bottles, thank you.' Lady Felicity Frumpton-Bumpton's lavishly decorated caravan is an exact replica of the fifth living room on the left from the entrance hall of Frumpton-Bumpton Manor. Don't laugh, the caravan of the future will look a lot like this. Like I said at the beginning of this chapter, the death of air travel will change how we take our holidays. Lady Felicity is going to want the same level of comfort on holiday as she's used to at home. And that means antique furniture, a roaring open fire and a butler never more than a few feet away. Even the proletariat will expect much more luxury in their caravans.

Rosaria Bulldoggia, Spain's foremost female bullfighter, poses in her costume at the door of her walnut-panelled luxury caravan.

the future

Caravanning becomes an addiction, whether you love caravans for their practicality, the challenge of towing them, the smell of damp plywood or, like me, you are hooked on watching them disintegrating as you sail through in a burning car.

As I said at the beginning of this chapter, caravanning is going to get more popular. Even places like Guernsey, which at the moment bans people from visiting the island by caravan (hang on, isn't that against our human rights?), will see sense and welcome the caravan. But it's time that caravan manufacturers started getting a bit more imaginative because the caravan hasn't really changed that much since The Wanderer. Except that we don't pull them by horse anymore or need men on tricycles going on ahead.

This caravan appears to have been made by toy-makers Fisher-Price, but why not experiment with different materials? That plastic looks great for resisting reversing errors.

This clever system uses energy from the solar panel to power a small electric motor, which in turn powers the small propeller on top of the mast. This gives the caravan and car extra performance.

It's about time some boffin in a white coat had a go at bringing the caravan more up to date. Surely a new material could be used – like the carbon fibre that's used on racing cars. Second thoughts, it's too strong to blow up.

The caravan loo, which we've recently looked closely at, though not too closely, is in dire need of modernisation. In the 21st century shouldn't we have something a little more advanced than a glorified bucket and a bottle of chemicals? Frankly, the situation stinks. Why not design a recycling potty that turns, er, waste into fuel? Actually, let's get off the subject right away.

Here's another variation on the wing-shaped caravan design complete with wing-shaped awning. Let's see some bolder ideas. How about a double-decker caravan?

The eco-caravan

Ha ha, you say, what on earth does Hammond know about greenness? He blows caravans up with super unleaded and high-grade rocket propellant. And he drives a filthy-dirty old 1960s Ford Mustang with a huge engine.

Well, this is where you're wrong. Just because I like the smell of gunpowder and love the sensation of crashing into caravans, it doesn't mean that I can't be interested in science and eco matters. In fact, I am.

The caravan has got a wonderful future in the eco-friendly world. Currently I help recycle caravans by blowing them up but in the future they could be made out of bio-degradable materials. Or even bio materials. Instead of plywood you could use a material grown from crops, such as crispbread. So when you've finished with your caravan I'll come along and spread it with cream cheese and then jump a car through it and eat the small pieces afterwards. Yum.

This experimental community living in giant Brie cheeses would do better to look at the good old caravan. Marginally less smelly than warm French cheese and considerably easier to move around. There's more standing room, too.

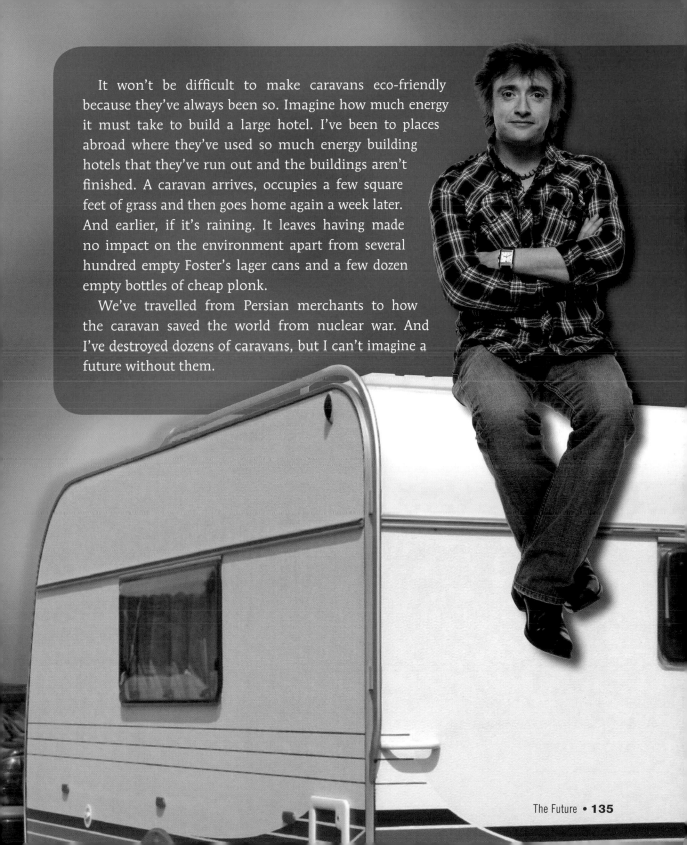

It won't be difficult to make caravans eco-friendly because they've always been so. Imagine how much energy it must take to build a large hotel. I've been to places abroad where they've used so much energy building hotels that they've run out and the buildings aren't finished. A caravan arrives, occupies a few square feet of grass and then goes home again a week later. And earlier, if it's raining. It leaves having made no impact on the environment apart from several hundred empty Foster's lager cans and a few dozen empty bottles of cheap plonk.

We've travelled from Persian merchants to how the caravan saved the world from nuclear war. And I've destroyed dozens of caravans, but I can't imagine a future without them.

Caravan jargon buster

All hobbies have their own vocabulary that's designed to trip up newcomers and make them feel complete Herberts. Nothing will advertise the fact that you're a caravan virgin more obviously than calling the loo a loo when it is in fact a 'head' or windows windows when they're portholes. But don't worry because I've compiled a list of caravan jargon and some short explanations. You'll never be afraid to go in the caravan site bathroom, sorry, toilet block, again.

Awning

A tent-like structure attached to the side of the caravan to give extra living space. Liable to self-destruct in high winds and direct Niagara-sized streams down your neck when it's raining.

Berth

A bunk or bed. Usually too short, too hard, too narrow or a combination of all three. A four-berth caravan sleeps four. At least that's what the manufacturer optimistically claims.

Breakaway cable

A short piece of metal cable that in the event of the caravan becoming detached from the tow vehicle pulls on the caravan's handbrake. A compulsory safety feature that will see your caravan neatly parked in the middle of the M5 while you arrive at your destination amazed by the speed of your car since passing Bristol.

Cassette toilet

A receptacle for holding old Val Doonican tapes or a toilet that can be emptied by removing a cassette from outside the caravan. Avoids tipping the contents of the chemical loo into auntie's beef casserole while carrying it through the caravan.

Corner steady

A jack system fitted to each corner of the caravan to keep it level on bumpy ground. Important for when the kids have been left at home.

Delamination

Also look under 'D for Disaster'. Delamination is when water gets into plywood and the layers start coming apart. Delamination also occurs when you place an anti-tank mine in a caravan and detonate it.

Dinette

Seating area that's usually too small and incorporates a table that is hard to put up but falls over easily.

Full service pitch

A pitch that has electricity hook-up, TV aerial, waste disposal and fresh water. The five-star hotel of pitches. Still no substitute for a real hotel.

Gross Train Weight

There are at least 87 different weight limits and measurements in caravanning and getting any one of them wrong will probably result in an accident. Gross Train Weight is the total weight of the car and caravan and should not exceed the maximums of both.

Jack-knife

A technique for closing all three lanes of a motorway on a bank holiday. Put simply, if you see a caravan towing a car down the road it's jacknifed. Usually results in buying a time share in southern Spain. Or divorce.

Hitch lock

Portly British film director famous for suspense thrillers such as *Pyscho*.

Jockey wheel

The small wheel that usually collapses when you're trying to manoeuvre the caravan when it's detached from the car. Named jockey because of its smallness, rather than for a win in the 2.30 at Kempton.

Noseweight

Not a piercing or the weight of a rock star's nose after he's been snorting the self-raising, but the weight that's pressing down on the tow vehicle's tow hitch. Important to get right. See 'Jack-knife'.

Outfit

Nerdy expression meaning the caravan and its tow vehicle. As in: 'That's a nice outfit you have there, Cuthbert.'

Rooflight

Perspex skylight that lets in water and amplifies the sound of rain drops.

Stabiliser

A device that goes between the tow bar and caravan that prevents excess wobble and snaking when towing. Like hangover cures, only partially effective.

Water carrier

Container that holds the caravans water supply if you're not on a Full Service Pitch. Is always empty late at night when it's raining.

On the right we have what is called a Mural. Generally applied using an airbrush and a healthy lack of taste and talent. You'll see murals on heavy lorries, usually German registered. Much rarer on caravans, thank goodness.

Richard Hammond is an award-winning television presenter whose wry and infectious humour first propelled him to fame in 2002 as one third of the *Top Gear* team. He has presented many other television series and documentaries, and co-developed a number of shows with his production company, Hamster's Wheel. He has written *What Not to Drive*; *Car Confidential*; *On the Edge*, the account of his near-fatal crash which was the number one non-fiction bestseller of 2007; *As You Do*, also a bestseller; and *On the Road*, a memoir of his early years, told in eight journeys. He has also destroyed more caravans than anyone else, anywhere.

Picture Credits

Every effort has been made to acknowledge all copyright holders as below and the publishers will, if notified, correct any errors in future editions.